Based on the **Hottest** New Word Craze

BANANAGRAMS!®

AN OFFICIAL BOOK

The ON-THE-GO Edition

TRAVEL
ADVENTURE
PUZZLE
PLAY
GAME
GO

MORE THAN 600 ALL-NEW PUZZLES

BY JOE EDLEY AND THE CREATORS OF BANANAGRAMS

The ON-THE-GO Edition

BANANA-GRAMS!®

AN OFFICIAL BOOK

BY JOE EDLEY

AND
THE CREATORS
OF

WORKMAN PUBLISHING • NEW YORK

Puzzles by Joe Edley

 Published simultaneously in Canada by Thomas Allen & Son Limited.

Library of Congress Cataloging-in-Publication Data

Edley, Joe.
Bananagrams! the on-the-go edition : more than 600 all-new word games / by Joe Edley.
p. cm.
ISBN 978-0-7611-6580-4 (alk. paper)
1. Word games. I. Title.
GV1507.W8E254 2011
793.734--dc23 2011024093

Workman books are available at special discounts when purchased in bulk for premiums and sales promotions as well as for fund-raising or educational use. Special editions or book excerpts also can be created to specification. For details, contact the Special Sales Director at the address below, or send an e-mail to specialmarkets@workman.com.

Design by Rae Ann Spitzenberger
Photo credit: felinda/fotolia

WORKMAN PUBLISHING COMPANY, INC.
225 Varick Street
New York, NY 10014-4381
www.workman.com

Printed in the United States of America
First printing August 2011

10 9 8 7 6 5 4 3 2 1

ON-THE-GO WELCOME TO BANANAGRAMS

THE STORY OF BANANAGRAMS

People have fallen hard for **Bananagrams,** the addictive craze that started as a simple idea: "An **anagram** game that is so fast it will drive you **bananas**!" And why not? It's amazingly fun and easy to play—you pick lettered tiles and create a grid of connecting and intersecting words as fast as you can.

It all began when three generations of our family were vacationing together on the beach. We wanted a game that everybody—no matter their age—could enjoy. After marathon sessions playing and experimenting with various permutations of word games, we ended up inventing Bananagrams. Our family was hooked—and so we decided to share our new creation with everyone. The next thing we knew the game was named Game of the Year. Not bad for a rainy-day invention.

We took it to the next level with *Bananagrams! The Official Book; More Bananagrams!;* then *10-Minute Bananagrams!* Now we're excited to present *Bananagrams! The On-the-Go Edition.*

Loaded with hundreds of new puzzles, this book promises a healthy dose of brain-twisting challenges in an extra-portable format.

We've continued our collaboration with Joe Edley, who is both a master Bananagrammer and the only three-time National Scrabble Champion in history. He's carefully crafted these smart and fast puzzles, which will thrill solvers of all stripes. So even if you've never grabbed a tile from a Bananagrams pouch, you're sure to find these puzzles very a-*peel*-ing!

HOW TO PLAY

Like the game, the puzzles in *Bananagrams! The On-the-Go Edition* are fast and fun. In all, there are 16 puzzle categories—some offer one big challenge, while others feature a group of shorter problems to solve. There are three levels of difficulty ranging from one banana (easy) to three bananas (hard). Dive in wherever you feel comfortable. If you're a beginner, you might try solving the puzzles with a pencil, in case you need to cross off tiles more than once. But if you're feeling brave, grab a pen!

All of the puzzles can be solved using common English words that appear in any standard dictionary. We've included a list of **Weords** (weird words!) on page 4 which we've compiled especially for Bananagrams players. This list features fun and unusual words that can come in very handy if you get stuck solving a puzzle. And just for fun, on page 13, you'll find a list of popular rule variations for new and clever ways to play Bananagrams, the game. Flip to the back of the book for the answer key, which starts on page 388. You'll notice that some of the puzzles have multiple solutions; in these cases the key gives only one of the many possible answers. If you find a different one, good for you—you've earned some bragging rights!

We hope you'll jump right in and start solving. Have fun and don't be surprised if these puzzles drive you bananas!

The Nathanson Family
Creators of Bananagrams

WEORDS!

These WEORDS (weird words!) are strange and useful words that can help you be a better Bananagrammer. Have a bunch of A s and O s and U s? Or maybe you need the perfect 3-letter word that starts with Y to finish your grid? These lists of handy and unusual words can help get you out of many a Bananagrams jam!

2-LETTER WORDS

AA	BE	FE	LO	OM	TI
AB	BI	GO	MA	ON	TO
AD	BO	HA	ME	OP	UH
AE	BY	HE	MI	OR	UM
AG	DE	HI	MM	OS	UN
AH	DO	HM	MO	OW	UP
AI	ED	HO	MU	OX	US
AL	EF	ID	MY	OY	UT
AM	EH	IF	NA	PA	WE
AN	EL	IN	NE	PE	WO
AR	EM	IS	NO	PI	XI
AS	EN	IT	NU	QI	XU
AT	ER	JO	OD	RE	YA
AW	ES	KA	OE	SH	YE
AX	ET	KI	OF	SI	YO
AY	EX	LA	OH	SO	ZA
BA	FA	LI	OI	TA	

3-LETTER WORDS

AAH
AAL
AAS
ABA
ABS
ABY
ACE
ACT
ADD
ADO
ADS
ADZ
AFF
AFT
AGA
AGE
AGO
AGS
AHA
AHI
AHS
AID
AIL
AIM
AIN
AIR
AIS
AIT
ALA
ALB
ALE
ALL
ALP
ALS
ALT
AMA
AMI
AMP
AMU
ANA
AND
ANE
ANI
ANT
ANY
APE
APO
APP
APT
ARB
ARC
ARE
ARF
ARK
ARM
ARS
ART
ASH
ASK
ASP
ASS
ATE
ATT
AUK
AVA
AVE
AVO
AWA
AWE
AWL
AWN
AXE
AYE
AYS
AZO
BAA
BAD
BAG
BAH
BAL
BAM
BAN
BAP
BAR
BAS
BAT
BAY
BED
BEE
BEG
BEL
BEN
BES
BET
BEY
BIB
BID
BIG
BIN
BIO
BIS
BIT
BIZ
BOA
BOB
BOD
BOG
BOO
BOP
BOS
BOT
BOW
BOX
BOY
BRA
BRO
BRR
BUB
BUD
BUG
BUM
BUN
BUR
BUS
BUT
BUY
BYE
BYS
CAB
CAD
CAM
CAN
CAP
CAR
CAT
CAW
CAY
CEE
CEL
CEP
CHI
CIG
CIS
COB
COD
COG
COL
CON
COO
COP
COR
COS
COT
COW
COX
COY
COZ
CRU
CRY
CUB
CUD
CUE
CUM
CUP
CUR
CUT
CWM
DAB
DAD
DAG
DAH
DAK
DAL
DAM
DAN
DAP
DAW
DAY
DEB
DEE

Did You Know?

• At the 1876 Philadelphia Centennial Exhibition, bananas were introduced to the American public. Deemed improper to eat from the peel, bananas were sliced, wrapped in foil, and sold for a dime.

DEF
DEL
DEN
DEV
DEW
DEX
DEY
DIB
DID
DIE
DIF
DIG
DIM
DIN
DIP
DIS
DIT
DOC
DOE
DOG
DOL
DOM
DON
DOR
DOS
DOT
DOW
DRY
DUB
DUD
DUE
DUG
DUH
DUN
DUO
DUP
DYE
EAR
EAT
EAU
EBB
ECU
EDH
EDS
EEK
EEL
EFF
EFS
EFT
EGG
EGO
EKE
ELD
ELF
ELK
ELL
ELM
ELS
EME
EMS
EMU
END
ENG
ENS
EON
ERA
ERE
ERG
ERN
ERR
ERS
ESS
ETA
ETH
EVE
EWE
EYE
FAB
FAD
FAN
FAR
FAS
FAT
FAX
FAY
FED
FEE
FEH
FEM
FEN
FER
FES
FET
FEU
FEW
FEY
FEZ
FIB
FID
FIE
FIG
FIL
FIN
FIR
FIT
FIX
FIZ
FLU
FLY
FOB
FOE
FOG
FOH
FON
FOP
FOR
FOU
FOX
FOY
FRO
FRY
FUB
FUD
FUG
FUN
FUR
GAB
GAD
GAE
GAG
GAL
GAM
GAN
GAP
GAR
GAS

GAT
GAY
GED
GEE
GEL
GEM
GEN
GET
GEY
GHI
GIB
GID
GIE
GIG
GIN
GIP
GIT
GNU
GOA
GOB
GOD
GOO
GOR
GOS
GOT
GOX
GUL
GUM
GUN
GUT
GUV
GUY
GYM
GYP
HAD
HAE
HAG
HAH
HAJ
HAM
HAO
HAP
HAS
HAT
HAW
HAY
HEH
HEM
HEN
HEP
HER
HES
HET
HEW
HEX
HEY
HIC
HID
HIE
HIM
HIN
HIP
HIS
HIT
HMM
HOB
HOD
HOE
HOG
HON
HOP
HOT
HOW
HOY
HUB
HUE
HUG
HUH
HUM
HUN
HUP
HUT
HYP
ICE
ICH
ICK
ICY
IDS
IFF
IFS
IGG
ILK
ILL
IMP
INK
INN
INS
ION
IRE
IRK
ISM
ITS
IVY
JAB
JAG
JAM
JAR
JAW
JAY
JEE
JET
JEU
JEW
JIB
JIG
JIN
JOB
JOE
JOG
JOT
JOW
JOY
JUG
JUN
JUS
JUT
KAB
KAE
KAF
KAS
KAT
KAY
KEA
KEF
KEG
KEN

Did You Know?

• Bananas have a reputation as a "radioactive fruit." Since they're rich in potassium, and one hundredth of one percent of the world's potassium atoms is radioactive, they have higher natural radioactivity than other fruits and veggies!

KEP
KEX
KEY
KHI
KID
KIF
KIN
KIP
KIR
KIS
KIT
KOA
KOB
KOI
KOP
KOR
KOS
KUE
KYE
LAB
LAC
LAD
LAG
LAM
LAP
LAR
LAS
LAT
LAV
LAW
LAX
LAY
LEA
LED
LEE
LEG
LEI
LEK
LES
LET
LEU
LEV
LEX
LEY
LIB
LID
LIE
LIN
LIP
LIS
LIT
LOB
LOG
LOO
LOP
LOT
LOW
LOX
LUG
LUM
LUV
LUX
LYE
MAC
MAD
MAE
MAG
MAN
MAP
MAR
MAS
MAT
MAW
MAX
MAY
MED
MEG
MEL
MEM
MEN
MET
MEW
MHO
MIB
MIC
MID
MIG
MIL
MIM
MIR
MIS
MIX
MOA
MOB
MOC
MOD
MOG
MOL
MOM
MON
MOO
MOP
MOR
MOS
MOT
MOW
MUD
MUG
MUM
MUN
MUS
MUT
MYC
NAB
NAE
NAG
NAH
NAM
NAN
NAP
NAW
NAY
NEB
NEE
NEG
NET
NEW
NIB
NIL
NIM
NIP
NIT
NIX
NOB
NOD
NOG
NOH
NOM
NOO
NOR
NOS
NOT
NOW
NTH
NUB
NUN
NUS
NUT
OAF
OAK
OAR
OAT
OBA
OBE
OBI
OCA
ODA
ODD
ODE
ODS
OES
OFF
OFT
OHM
OHO
OHS
OIL
OKA
OKE
OLD
OLE
OMS
ONE
ONO
ONS
OOH
OOT
OPE
OPS
OPT
ORA
ORB
ORC
ORE
ORS
OSE
OUD
OUR
OUT
OVA
OWE
OWL

OWN
OXO
OXY
PAC
PAD
PAH
PAL
PAM
PAN
PAP
PAR
PAS
PAT
PAW
PAX
PAY
PEA
PEC
PED
PEE
PEG
PEH
PEN
PEP
PER
PES
PET
PEW
PHI
PHT
PIA
PIC
PIE
PIG
PIN
PIP
PIS
PIT
PIU
PIX
PLY
POD
POH
POI
POL
POO
POP
POT
POW
POX
PRO
PRY
PSI
PST
PUB
PUD
PUG
PUL
PUN
PUP
PUR
PUS
PUT
PYA
PYE
PYX
QAT
QIS
QUA
RAD
RAG
RAH
RAI
RAJ
RAM
RAN
RAP
RAS
RAT
RAW
RAX
RAY
REB
REC
RED
REE
REF
REG
REI
REM
REP
RES
RET
REV
REX
RHO

Did You Know?

• Uganda has the highest average consumption of bananas in the world—about 500 pounds of the fruit, per person, per year! In fact, in their language, *matooke*, which means "food," also means "banana."

RIA
RIB
RID
RIF
RIG
RIM
RIN
RIP
ROB
ROC
ROD
ROE
ROM
ROT
ROW
RUB
RUE
RUG
RUM
RUN
RUT
RYA
RYE
SAB
SAC
SAD
SAE
SAG
SAL
SAP
SAT
SAU
SAW
SAX
SAY
SEA

SEC
SEE
SEG
SEI
SEL
SEN
SER
SET
SEW
SEX
SHA
SHE
SHH
SHY
SIB
SIC
SIM
SIN
SIP
SIR
SIS
SIT
SIX
SKA
SKI
SKY
SLY
SOB
SOD
SOL
SOM
SON
SOP
SOS
SOT
SOU
SOW
SOX
SOY
SPA
SPY
SRI
STY
SUB
SUE
SUK
SUM
SUN
SUP
SUQ
SYN
TAB
TAD
TAE
TAG
TAJ
TAM
TAN
TAO
TAP
TAR
TAS
TAT
TAU
TAV
TAW
TAX
TEA
TED
TEE
TEG
TEL
TEN
TET
TEW
THE
THO
THY
TIC
TIE
TIL
TIN
TIP
TIS
TIT
TOD
TOE
TOG
TOM
TON
TOO
TOP
TOR
TOT
TOW
TOY
TRY
TSK
TUB
TUG
TUI
TUN
TUP
TUT
TUX
TWA
TWO
TYE
UDO
UGH
UKE
ULU
UMM
UMP
UNS
UPO
UPS
URB
URD
URN
URP
USE
UTA
UTE
UTS
VAC
VAN
VAR
VAS
VAT
VAU
VAV
VAW
VEE
VEG
VET
VEX
VIA
VID
VIE
VIG
VIM
VIS
VOE
VOW
VOX
VUG
VUM
WAB
WAD
WAE
WAG
WAN
WAP
WAR
WAS
WAT
WAW
WAX
WAY
WEB
WED
WEE
WEN
WET
WHA
WHO
WHY
WIG
WIN
WIS
WIT
WIZ
WOE
WOK
WON
WOO
WOS
WOT
WOW
WRY
WUD
WYE
WYN
XIS
YAG
YAH
YAK
YAM
YAP
YAR
YAW

YAY
YEA
YEH
YEN
YEP
YES
YET
YEW
YIN
YIP
YOB
YOD
YOK
YOM
YON
YOU
YOW
YUK
YUM
YUP
ZAG
ZAP
ZAS
ZAX
ZED
ZEE
ZEK
ZEP
ZIG
ZIN
ZIP
ZIT
ZOA
ZOO
ZUZ
ZZZ

WORDS WITH A LOT OF VOWELS

AA
AALII
ADIEU
AE
AECIA
AEON
AERIE
AERO
AGEE
AGIO
AGUE
AI
AIDE
AIOLI
AJEE
AKEE
ALAE
ALEE
ALOE
AMIA
AMIE
ANOA
AQUA
AREA
ARIA
ASEA
AUDIO
AURA
AURAE
AUREI
AUTO
AWEE
BEAU
CIAO
EASE
EAU
EAUX
EAVE
EERIE
EIDE
EMEU
EPEE
ETUI
EURO
IDEA
ILEA
ILIA
INIA
IOTA
IXIA
JIAO
LIEU
LOUIE
LUAU
MEOU
MIAOU
MOUE
OBIA
OBOE
OE
OGEE
OI
OIDIA
OLEA
OLEO
OLIO
OORIE
OOZE
OURIE
OUZO
QUAI
QUEUE
ROUE
TOEA
UNAI
UNAU
URAEI
UREA
UVEA
ZOEA
ZOEAE

WORDS WITH NO VOWELS

BRR
BY(S)
CRWTH
CRY
CRYPT(S)
CWM
CYST(S)
DRY(S)
DRYLY
FLY
FLYBY(S)
FLYSCH

FRY
GHYLL(S)
GLYCYL(S)
GLYPH(S)
GYM(S)
GYP(S)
GYPSY
HM
HMM
HYMN(S)
HYP(S)
LYMPH(S)
LYNCH
LYNX
MM
MY
MYC(S)
MYRRH(S)
MYTH(S)
MYTHY
NTH
NYMPH(S)
PLY
PRY
PST
PSYCH(S)
PYGMY
PYX
RHYTHM(S)
RYND(S)
SCRY
SH
SHY
SHYLY
SKY
SLY
SLYLY
SPRY
SPRYLY
SPY
STY
STYMY
SYLPH(S)
SYLPHY
SYN
SYNC(S)
SYNCH(S)
SYNTH(S)
SYPH(S)
SYZYGY
THY
THYMY
TRY
TRYST(S)
TSK
TYPP(S)
TYPY
WHY(S)
WRY
WRYLY
WYCH
WYN(S)
WYND(S)
WYNN(S)
XYLYL(S)
XYST(S)
ZZZ

Q WORDS WITH NO U

FAQIR(S)
MBAQANGA(S)
QABALA(S)
QABALAH(S)
QADI(S)
QAID(S)
QANAT(S)
QAT(S)
QI
QINDAR(S)
QINDARKA
QINTAR(S)
QIS
QOPH(S)
QWERTY(S)
SHEQALIM
SHEQEL(S)
TRANQ(S)

OTHER WAYS TO PLAY

Those of you who love to play Bananagrams, the game, know that playing it is fast and easy. You pick lettered tiles and compete against other players to create grids of connecting and intersecting words that use up all of your tiles. For all of you who've mastered the basic Bananagrams game and are itching for new ways to play, we're including some popular variations of the game that will help you hone your skills and put you on your way to being an expert Bananagrammer!

BANANA SMOOTHIE

To play this less hectic version of the game, place all of the tiles facedown and divide them equally among the players. Play as you would a regular Bananagrams game, except instead of peeling or dumping, each player uses only the tiles they've already been given. The first player to use up all of their letters says "Bananas!" and is the winner. If the game ends in a stalemate, the player with the fewest remaining tiles wins.

BANANA SOLITAIRE

To play the game by yourself, place all of the tiles facedown on the table. Take 21 tiles and play the game as you normally would. Only peel when you've used up your existing tiles. See how long it takes you to use up all 144 tiles, and then try to beat your own best time. Or challenge yourself by trying to make as few words as you can with all 144 letters.

BANANA CAFÉ

To play this version—which is perfect for playing in restaurants—place the Bananagrams pouch on the table. Each player takes 21 tiles from the pouch. Play as you would a regular Bananagrams game, except no peeling is allowed. (You are allowed to dump tiles.) The first player to use up all of their letters says "Bananas!" and is the winner. If the game ends in a stalemate, the player with the fewest remaining tiles wins.

BEST BANANA

Divide the tiles evenly among all players. Then, instead of making word grids, have each player try to spell the longest word they can using the tiles they have. Give points for the longest word. Instead of finding the longest word, you can make this a contest to spell the most words, the most unusual words, or even the all-around best words (though judging these can often turn into quite a battle!).

BANANAS ON BOARD

Play the game as you normally would, except limit the sprawl of the word grids. For instance, you could say that each player's grid must fit into a 10×10 tile space, or you could rip out sheets of notepaper and use them as boards. This forces a more condensed playing area and makes it more challenging to find words that fit.

BANANA CLUES

Play the game as you normally would. Once everyone has finished, each player writes out a clue for every word that appears in their grid. Then everyone passes their clue sheet and their bunch of mixed-up tiles to the player on their right. Using the tiles and clue sheet that were passed to them, each player must try to recreate the grid that the original player formed.

BANANA THEMES

In this version, all of the rules for a regular game of Bananagrams apply. However, instead of spelling any words they can, players must include in their word grid at least one word related to a given theme. To make this even more challenging, require players to use two or three (or more!) words that relate to the theme. Here are some fun ideas for themes: names of family members, friends, or famous people; objects in the room; holiday words; animals; sports; clothing; winter, spring, summer, or fall words; buildings; parts of the body; school; politics; nature; words related to a specific movie, TV show, or book.

BANANA NUMBERS

In this version, all of the rules for a regular game of Bananagrams apply. However, instead of spelling any words they can, players must only spell a certain number of words or words that are of a certain length. For instance, you could say that each player can only have four words in his or her grid. Or you could say that each player must only use words that are four letters long. The longer the words or the fewer words allowed in a grid, the harder the game.

The ON-THE-GO Edition
BANANAGRAMS!®

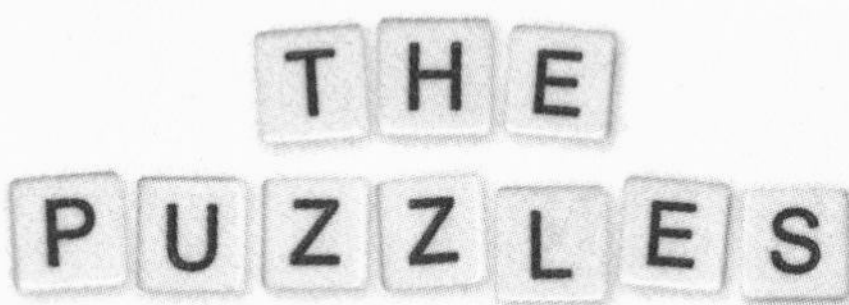

For each of the word groups below, change one letter in the top word to one of the letters that appears in the bottom word, then rearrange the tiles to form a new common word. Do the same with each new word until you arrive at the bottom word.

For example, one path from BARK to PLUM is BARK, MARK, RAMP, RUMP, PLUM.

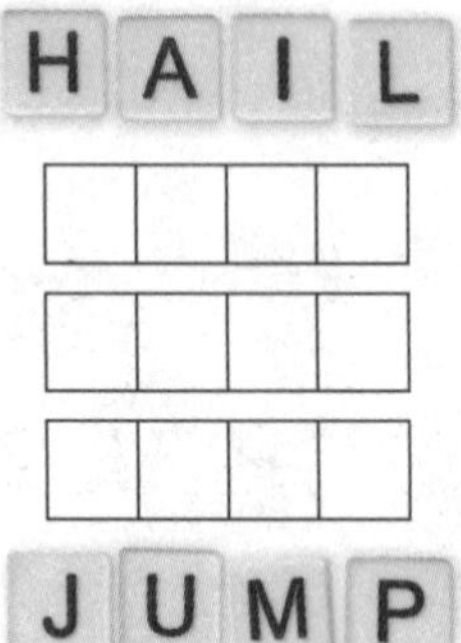

BUNCH OF BANANAS

For each word or phrase below, rearrange the letters to spell two things that are black. For example, A BOILER can be rearranged to spell BEAR, OIL. The first letter of each word is placed to get you started.

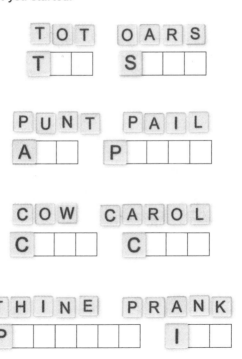

TOT OARS

T _ _ S _ _ _

PUNT PAIL

A _ _ P _ _ _ _

COW CAROL

C _ _ _ C _ _ _

THINE PRANK

P _ _ _ _ _ _ I _ _

For each bunch below, rearrange the letters to form two intersecting words that fit into the corresponding grid.

A A D E I M T U V

A D E E H I L U V

Each of the words below can be turned into another word on the list by changing one letter and then rearranging them all to form a new word. For example, REGIMENT can be turned into STEERING by changing the M to an S, so they would be a pair. How quickly can you find all the pairs?

1. AMEBA
2. ACTOR
3. BAAED
4. COBRA
5. BEGAT
6. REHAB
7. TOGAE
8. BRAVE

Pairs

___ ___

___ ___

___ ___

___ ___

BANANA CRUNCH

Each set of ten tiles contains two common five-letter words. The letters of the first five-letter word are adjacent, but not in order. Find them and rearrange them to spell a word. Cross out those letters and rearrange the five remaining letters to spell the second word.

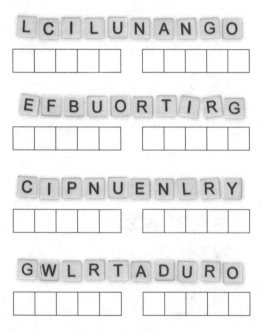

L C I L U N A N G O

E F B U O R T I R G

C I P N U E N L R Y

G W L R T A D U R O

Rearrange the letters of each word below and place them in the blanks so that, together with the two letters that have already been placed, they form a new word.

Use the 15 tiles in this bunch to create words that fit into the grids below. To get you started, a few tiles from the bunch have been placed in the grid. The BANANA BITES provide hints for one word to help you solve each grid. Reuse the 15 tiles in the bunch for each grid.

A I O B O E R
J B L S E L T T

B L
T

1. **BANANA BITE:** Employment

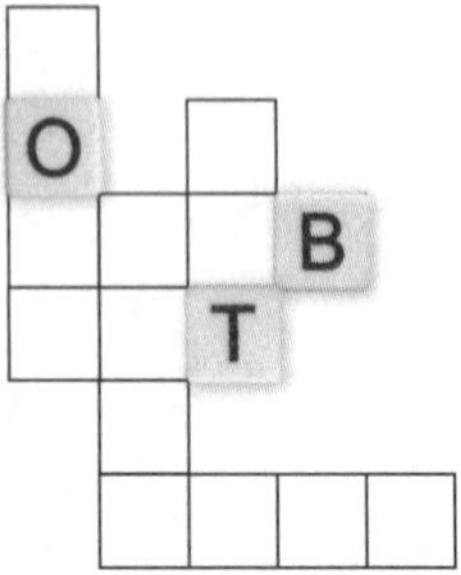

O
B
T

2. **BANANA BITE:** Word game playing piece

BANANA SHAKES

LEVEL

Each of the following six-letter sets can be rearranged to spell out a common word that either starts with BR, CR, or DR or ends with AL, LE, or TE. Find all the words as quickly as you can.

A B E R R V

A C E L L O

A E G R T Y

A C N O R Y

A A C I L R

A E L S T U

A B C H O R

D H I R S Y

LEVEL

Add a D to each of the words below and then rearrange the letters in each word to form a new six-letter word.

BANANA PUDDING

LEVEL

Each of the two-letter groups below may be extended on both the right and the left to form a six-letter word. Drawing from the tiles directly above each group, fill in the blanks to find the words as quickly as you can.

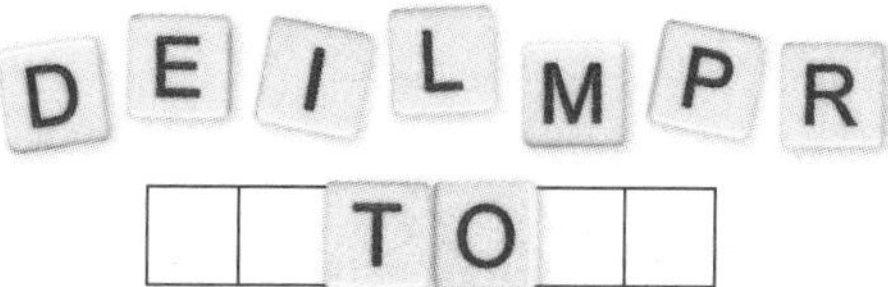

In each puzzle, use three of the tiles from the bunch to fill in the blanks and make a six-letter word that connects the grid.

C E A N O P T

ARM
FUN
ODOR

MILK
STAR
ASKEW

A H C L N O U

Each set of letters is arranged alphabetically. The ? is in the correct alphabetical position. Figure out what letter the ? represents and rearrange the letters to spell a six-letter word that begins with the given letter. For example, in A?ENTV the ? could be an A, B, C, D, or E. Here it represents a D, which can be combined with the other letters to spell ADVENT.

A E G I ? N

E _ _ _ _ _

A A H P ? Y

A _ _ _ _ _

B I ? R S T

B _ _ _ _ _

A E E G S ?

S _ _ _ _ _

There is one letter that when added to all of the four-letter words below can be used to form new five-letter words. Find the letter that works for all four words, add it to each word, and then rearrange each set of letters to form a new word. For example, B can be added to LOSS, ONLY, AUTO, and IRON to form SLOBS, NOBLY, ABOUT, and ROBIN.

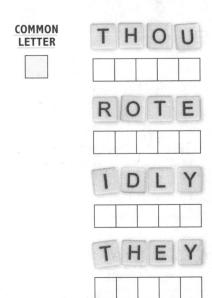

COMMON LETTER

☐

T H O U

☐☐☐☐☐

R O T E

☐☐☐☐☐

I D L Y

☐☐☐☐☐

T H E Y

☐☐☐☐☐

For each of the words below, replace one letter with the tile after the plus sign. Then rearrange the letters to spell a type of job.

N E A R L Y + W

C O D G E R + R

C L I P T + O

Rearrange the tiles below to spell a five-letter word that fits in the first row. Then drop one letter and rearrange the remaining tiles to spell a four-letter word in the next row. Continue dropping one letter until you complete all four words. To get you started, one tile has been placed in each row.

Using each two- and three-letter word just once, combine a word in the left column with a word in the right column. Then rearrange each five-letter scramble to form a word that begins with an A, E, or L and write it into the appropriate space below.

E N	O A F
P A	C A T
L O	E L L

A _ _ _ _

E _ _ _ _

L _ _ _ _

For each of the word groups below, change one letter in the top word to one of the letters that appears in the bottom word, then rearrange the tiles to form a new common word. Do the same with each new word until you arrive at the bottom word.

For example, one path from BARK to PLUM is BARK, MARK, RAMP, RUMP, PLUM.

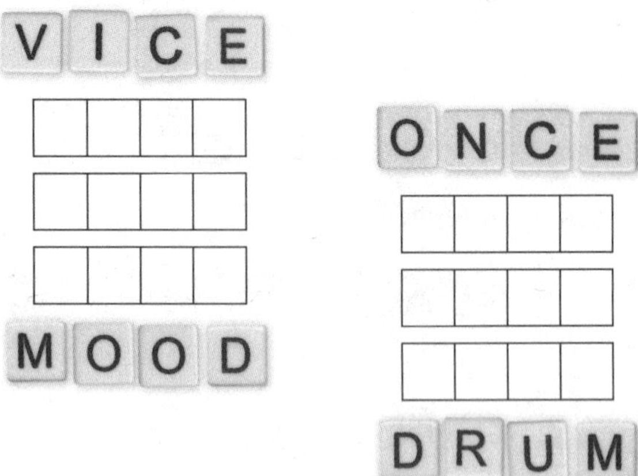

BUNCH OF BANANAS

For each word or phrase below, rearrange the letters to spell two things that are synonyms for "big." For example, MEDIC COPES can be rearranged to spell COSMIC, DEEP. The first letter of each word is placed to get you started.

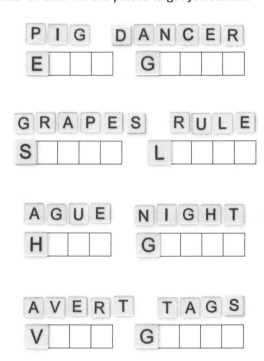

PIG DANCER

E _ _ _ G _ _ _ _

GRAPES RULE

S _ _ _ _ L _ _ _ _

AGUE NIGHT

H _ _ _ G _ _ _ _

AVERT TAGS

V _ _ _ G _ _ _ _

For each bunch below, rearrange the letters to form two intersecting words that fit into the corresponding grid.

A C F I R R T T R

B A B K O O L P T

Each of the words below can be turned into another word on the list by changing one letter and then rearranging them all to form a new word. For example, REGIMENT can be turned into STEERING by changing the M to an S, so they would be a pair. How quickly can you find all the pairs?

1. CAMEL
2. OAKEN
3. MAGIC
4. CANOE
5. VOCAL
6. HAVOC
7. ACING
8. LEMMA

Pairs

___ ___

___ ___

___ ___

___ ___

LEVEL

Each set of ten tiles contains two common five-letter words. The letters of the first five-letter word are adjacent, but not in order. Find them and rearrange them to spell a word. Cross out those letters and rearrange the five remaining letters to spell the second word.

H D I K S D A E A P

Y E A U E P S P A E

G A M C C A O O E I

O L E E B V D U H G

Rearrange the letters of each word below and place them in the blanks so that, together with the two letters that have already been placed, they form a new word.

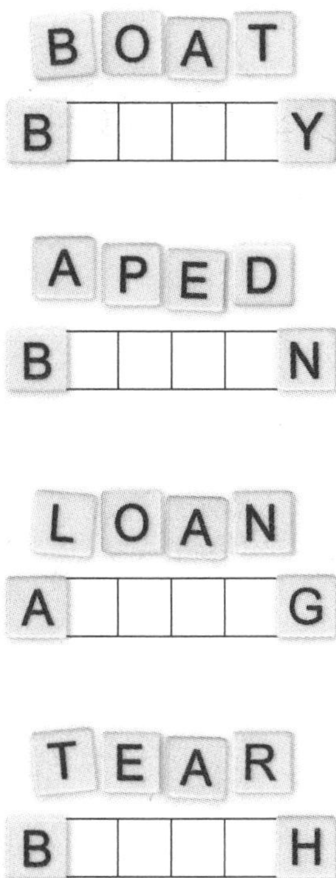

Use the 15 tiles in this bunch to create words that fit into the grids below. To get you started, a few tiles from the bunch have been placed in the grid. The BANANA BITES provide hints for one word to help you solve each grid. Reuse the 15 tiles in the bunch for each grid.

A M E I R T E

D H A N E L X Y

2. **BANANA BITE:** Built

E A

E

D

T

Y

1. **BANANA BITE:** Look at

M E

T

Each of the following six-letter sets can be rearranged to spell out a common word that either starts with CH, DE, or EN or ends with ED, LY, or ND. Find all the words as quickly as you can.

B C E H R U

B D E I M U

E L L N O R

A D G L L Y

C E E H S Y

B D E E N O

B L M M U Y

D E E G L N

Add a G to each of the words below and then rearrange the letters in each word to form a new six-letter word.

Each of the two-letter groups below may be extended on both the right and the left to form a six-letter word. Drawing from the tiles directly above each group, fill in the blanks to find the words as quickly as you can.

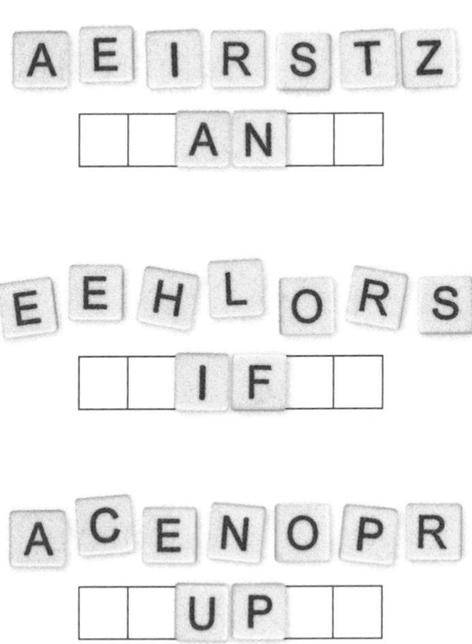

BANANA LEAVES

In each puzzle, use three of the tiles from the bunch to fill in the blanks and make a six-letter word that connects the grid.

Each set of letters is arranged alphabetically. The ? is in the correct alphabetical position. Figure out what letter the ? represents and rearrange the letters to spell a six-letter word that begins with the given letter. For example, in A?ENTV the ? could be an A, B, C, D, or E. Here it represents a D, which can be combined with the other letters to spell ADVENT.

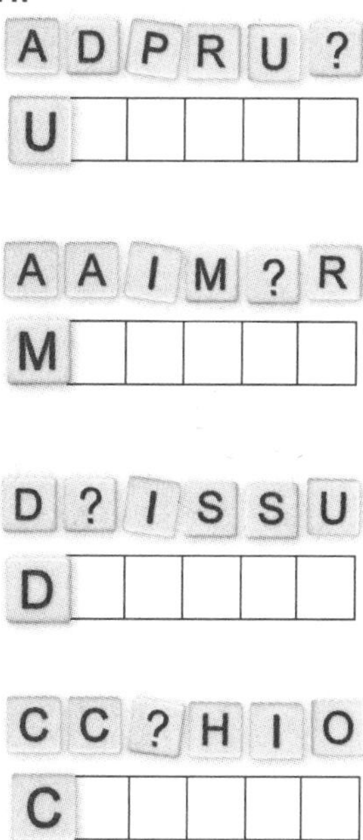

There is one letter that when added to all of the four-letter words below can be used to form new five-letter words. Find the letter that works for all four words, add it to each word, and then rearrange each set of letters to form a new word. For example, B can be added to LOSS, ONLY, AUTO, and IRON to form SLOBS, NOBLY, ABOUT, and ROBIN.

COMMON LETTER

UNIT

TRUE

WARN

SIRS

For each of the words below, replace one letter with the tile after the plus sign. Then rearrange the letters to spell a basketball term.

N E E D L E S + F

T R A N C E + E

C L O A K + B

Rearrange the tiles below to spell a five-letter word that fits in the first row. Then drop one letter and rearrange the remaining tiles to spell a four-letter word in the next row. Continue dropping one letter until you complete all four words. To get you started, one tile has been placed in each row.

Using each two- and three-letter word just once, combine a word in the left column with a word in the right column. Then rearrange each five-letter scramble to form a word that begins with a B, G, or H and write it into the appropriate space below.

LO	GUN
AT	RIB
MI	DUH

B _ _ _ _

G _ _ _ _

H _ _ _ _

For each of the word groups below, change one letter in the top word to one of the letters that appears in the bottom word, then rearrange the tiles to form a new common word. Do the same with each new word until you arrive at the bottom word.

For example, one path from BARK to PLUM is BARK, MARK, RAMP, RUMP, PLUM.

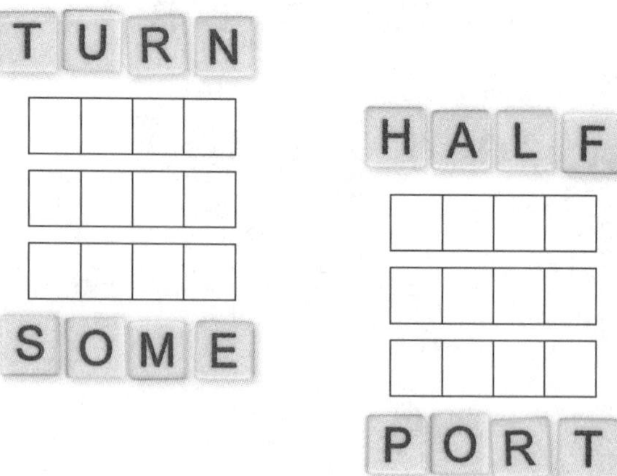

BUNCH OF BANANAS

For each word or phrase below, rearrange the letters to spell two common boy's names. For example, CHARM SIS can be rearranged to spell CHRIS, SAM. The first letter of each word is placed to get you started.

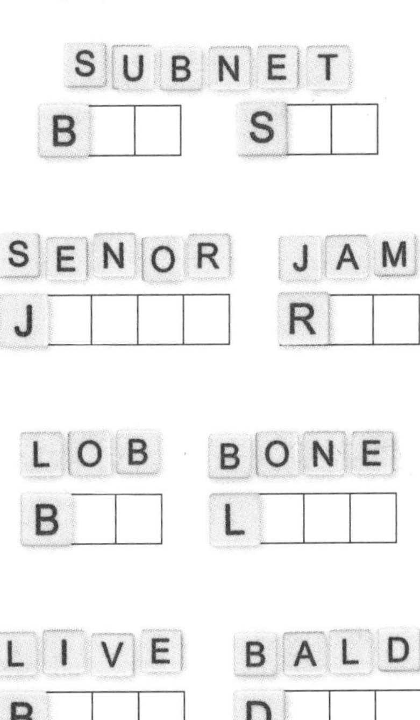

For each bunch below, rearrange the letters to form two intersecting words that fit into the corresponding grid.

A D G K N T W Y U

A B C K O T O U W

Each of the words below can be turned into another word on the list by changing one letter and then rearranging them all to form a new word. For example, REGIMENT can be turned into STEERING by changing the M to an S, so they would be a pair. How quickly can you find all the pairs?

1. YACHT
2. RATIO
3. SAUCY
4. TEACH
5. SCUBA
6. ADIEU
7. COATI
8. GUIDE

Pairs

___ ___

___ ___

___ ___

___ ___

LEVEL

Each set of ten tiles contains two common five-letter words. The letters of the first five-letter word are adjacent, but not in order. Find them and rearrange them to spell a word. Cross out those letters and rearrange the five remaining letters to spell the second word.

T T E R C P U B T E

U L N T O F E T V A

I L E F O R Y U T B

C E R R D A A T T O

Rearrange the letters of each word below and place them in the blanks so that, together with the two letters that have already been placed, they form a new word.

Use the 15 tiles in this bunch to create words that fit into the grids below. To get you started, a few tiles from the bunch have been placed in the grid. The BANANA BITES provide hints for one word to help you solve each grid. Reuse the 15 tiles in the bunch for each grid.

C R O E I M N
I E N G U G T Z

M E
R
N

1. **BANANA BITE:**
Healing

N
C I
G

2. **BANANA BITE:**
Joining

Each of the following six-letter sets can be rearranged to spell out a common word that either starts with BI, CO, or GR or ends with NE, TY, or VE. Find all the words as quickly as you can.

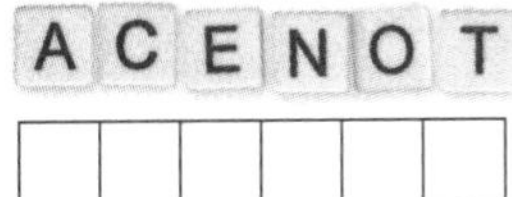

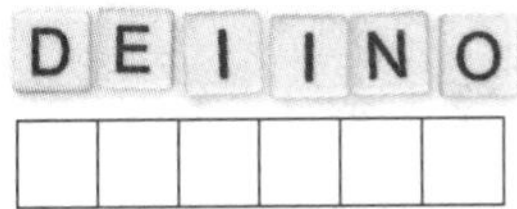

Add a N to each of the words below and then rearrange the letters in each word to form a new six-letter word.

Each of the two-letter groups below may be extended on both the right and the left to form a six-letter word. Drawing from the tiles directly above each group, fill in the blanks to find the words as quickly as you can.

BANANA LEAVES

LEVEL

In each puzzle, use three of the tiles from the bunch to fill in the blanks and make a six-letter word that connects the grid.

A H C I L M U

BOTH
ATOM
HELP

GUT
LEAN
SKATE

B E D K L R T

Each set of letters is arranged alphabetically. The ? is in the correct alphabetical position. Figure out what letter the ? represents and rearrange the letters to spell a six-letter word that begins with the given letter. For example, in A?ENTV the ? could be an A, B, C, D, or E. Here it represents a D, which can be combined with the other letters to spell ADVENT.

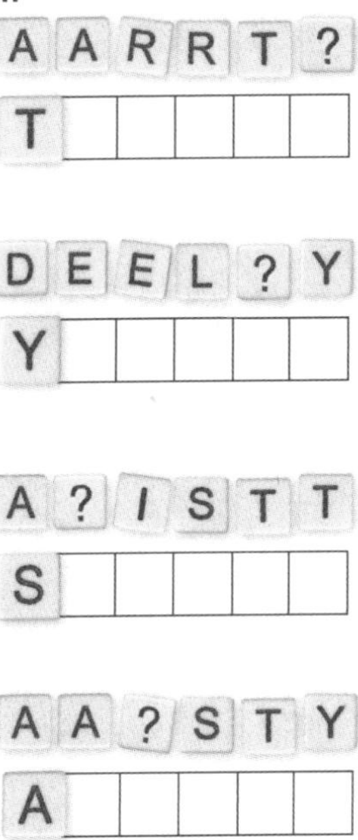

There is one letter that when added to all of the four-letter words below can be used to form new five-letter words. Find the letter that works for all four words, add it to each word, and then rearrange each set of letters to form a new word. For example, B can be added to LOSS, ONLY, AUTO, and IRON to form SLOBS, NOBLY, ABOUT, and ROBIN.

COMMON LETTER

☐

P E R T

☐☐☐☐☐

H E R S

☐☐☐☐☐

T E E N

☐☐☐☐☐

F R E E

☐☐☐☐☐

TOTALLY BANANAS

For each of the words below, replace one letter with the tile after the plus sign. Then rearrange the letters to spell something that is often bright.

S L I D E + M

T H I N G + L

M E D I A + S

M E T A L + F

Rearrange the tiles below to spell a five-letter word that fits in the first row. Then drop one letter and rearrange the remaining tiles to spell a four-letter word in the next row. Continue dropping one letter until you complete all four words. To get you started, one tile has been placed in each row.

Using each two- and three-letter word just once, combine a word in the left column with a word in the right column. Then rearrange each five-letter scramble to form a word that begins with an S, W, or Y and write it into the appropriate space below.

HA	COT
UH	TOY
US	WET

S _ _ _ _

W _ _ _ _

Y _ _ _ _

LEVEL

For each of the word groups below, change one letter in the top word to one of the letters that appears in the bottom word, then rearrange the tiles to form a new common word. Do the same with each new word until you arrive at the bottom word.

For example, one path from BARK to PLUM is BARK, MARK, RAMP, RUMP, PLUM.

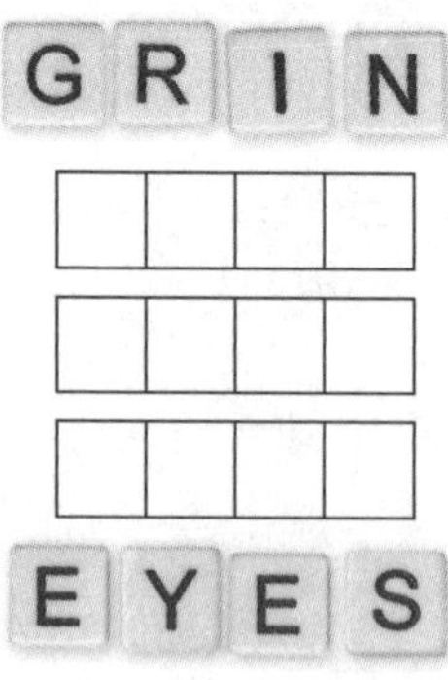

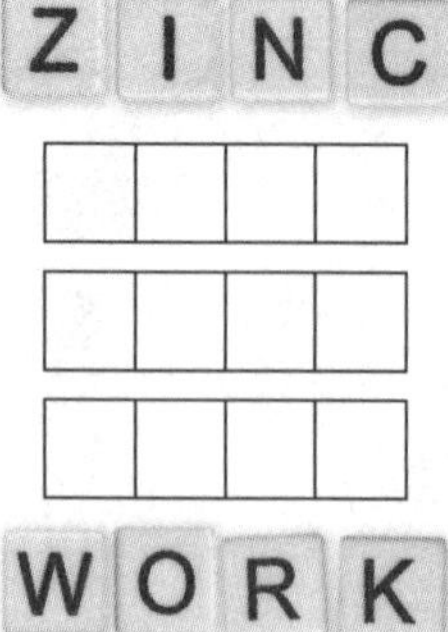

BUNCH OF BANANAS

LEVEL

For each word or phrase below, rearrange the letters to spell two things that are opposite in meaning. For example, FILL EARS can be rearranged to spell FALL, RISE. The first letter of each word is placed to get you started.

TRASH FLAP

S _ _ _ _ F _ _ _

PRO CHOIR

R _ _ _ P _ _ _

SAD TINTS

S _ _ S _ _ _ _

HAIL DATE

H _ _ _ T _ _ _

For each bunch below, rearrange the letters to form two intersecting words that fit into the corresponding grid.

A G I M O R V X Y

A C C F I H O R Y

Each of the words below can be turned into another word on the list by changing one letter and then rearranging them all to form a new word. For example, REGIMENT can be turned into STEERING by changing the M to an S, so they would be a pair. How quickly can you find all the pairs?

1. ADMIT
2. ACIDS
3. WOULD
4. ADOPT
5. DAISY
6. TIDAL
7. ALOUD
8. TODAY

Pairs

____ ____

____ ____

____ ____

____ ____

LEVEL

Each set of ten tiles contains two common five-letter words. The letters of the first five-letter word are adjacent, but not in order. Find them and rearrange them to spell a word. Cross out those letters and rearrange the five remaining letters to spell the second word.

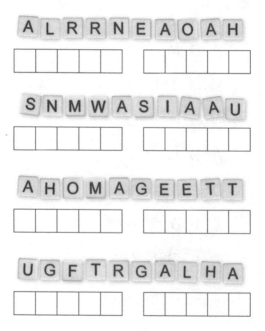

A L R R N E A O A H

S N M W A S I A A U

A H O M A G E E T T

U G F T R G A L H A

Rearrange the letters of each word below and place them in the blanks so that, together with the two letters that have already been placed, they form a new word.

Use the 15 tiles in this bunch to create words that fit into the grids below. To get you started, a few tiles from the bunch have been placed in the grid. The BANANA BITES provide hints for one word to help you solve each grid. Reuse the 15 tiles in the bunch for each grid.

A O I P U S T
F E S T K R W U

1. **BANANA BITE:** Drinking container opening

2. **BANANA BITE:** Baseball grounds

Each of the following six-letter sets can be rearranged to spell out a common word that either starts with GL, HE, or IN or ends with AN, EN, or ON. Find all the words as quickly as you can.

A B C E N O

A B N R T U

A E H H L T

A M N O R T

A C I N T T

E I N R T V

C G H I L T

D D E H I N

Add an L to each of the words below and then rearrange the letters in each word to form a new six-letter word.

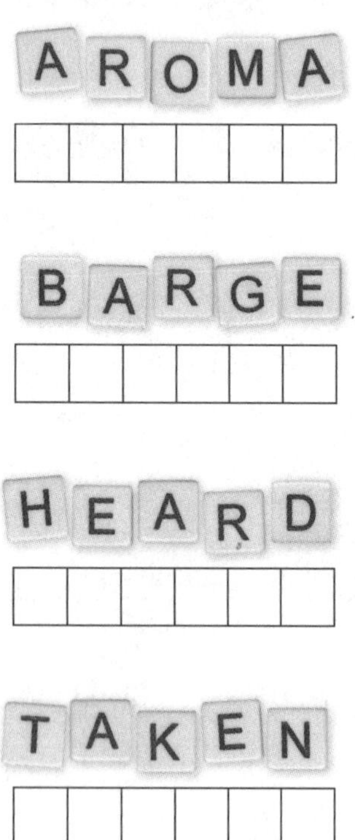

BANANA PUDDING

LEVEL

Each of the two-letter groups below may be extended on both the right and the left to form a six-letter word. Drawing from the tiles directly above each group, fill in the blanks to find the words as quickly as you can.

In each puzzle, use three of the tiles from the bunch to fill in the blanks and make a six-letter word that connects the grid.

E F A N R S Y

	☐		
E	D	I	T
	☐		
B	I	N	D
	☐		
I	T	E	M

	☐			
C	H	A	P	
	☐			
Z	O	N	E	
	☐			
S	T	O	N	E

A I C L P R T

Each set of letters is arranged alphabetically. The ? is in the correct alphabetical position. Figure out what letter the ? represents and rearrange the letters to spell a six-letter word that begins with the given letter. For example, in A?ENTV the ? could be an A, B, C, D, or E. Here it represents a D, which can be combined with the other letters to spell ADVENT.

There is one letter that when added to all of the four-letter words below can be used to form new five-letter words. Find the letter that works for all four words, add it to each word, and then rearrange each set of letters to form a new word. For example, B can be added to LOSS, ONLY, AUTO, and IRON to form SLOBS, NOBLY, ABOUT, and ROBIN.

COMMON LETTER

☐

T R I M

☐☐☐☐☐

B U Y S

☐☐☐☐☐

G O U T

☐☐☐☐☐

G I F T

☐☐☐☐☐

TOTALLY BANANAS

LEVEL

For each of the words below, replace one letter with the tile after the plus sign. Then rearrange the letters to spell a type of shape.

P E S T E R + H

N O T E D + U

O M E N + C

L I T H E + X

Rearrange the tiles below to spell a five-letter word that fits in the first row. Then drop one letter and rearrange the remaining tiles to spell a four-letter word in the next row. Continue dropping one letter until you complete all four words. To get you started, one tile has been placed in each row.

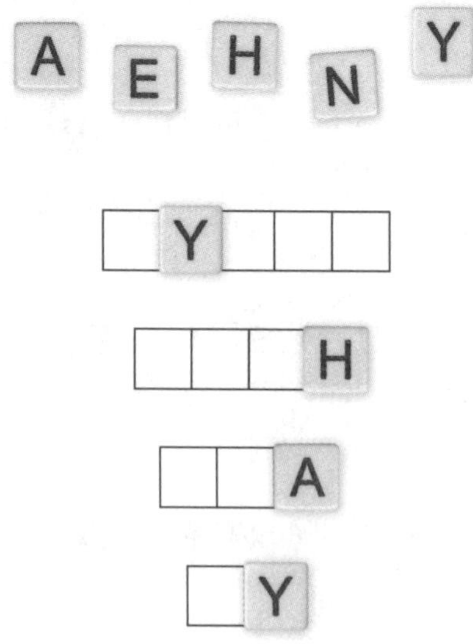

Using each two- and three-letter word just once, combine a word in the left column with a word in the right column. Then rearrange each five-letter scramble to form a word that begins with an F, R, or T and write it into the appropriate space below.

OF	SUE
WE	TEN
RE	OIL

F _ _ _ _

R _ _ _ _

T _ _ _ _

For each of the word groups below, change one letter in the top word to one of the letters that appears in the bottom word, then rearrange the tiles to form a new common word. Do the same with each new word until you arrive at the bottom word.

For example, one path from BARK to PLUM is BARK, MARK, RAMP, RUMP, PLUM.

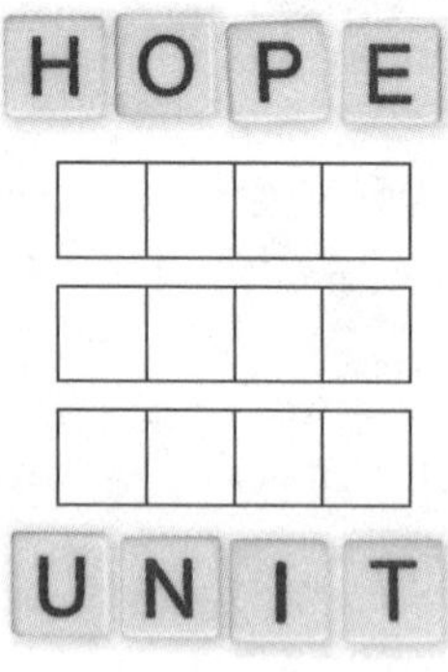

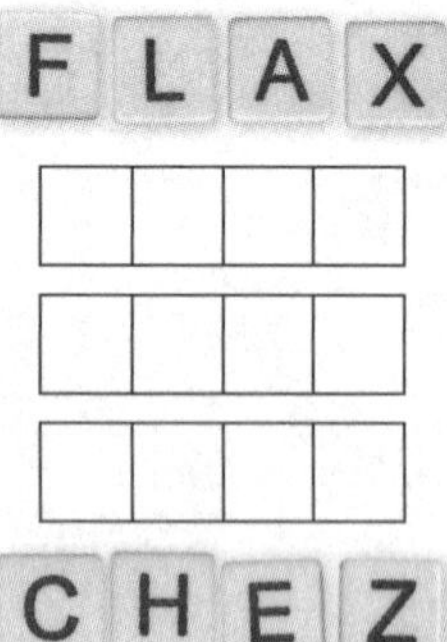

BUNCH OF BANANAS

LEVEL

For each word or phrase below, rearrange the letters to spell two things that are types of water vehicles. For example, JOB GRIEF TALE can be rearranged to spell BARGE, JETFOIL. The first letter of each word is placed to get you started.

BIG TOY HAND

D _ _ _ _ _   B _ _ _

AN OKAY CAKE

C _ _ _ _   K _ _ _ _

I HATCH SPY

S _ _ _   Y _ _ _ _

REF TRY ARF

R _ _ _   F _ _ _ _

For each bunch below, rearrange the letters to form two intersecting words that fit into the corresponding grid.

A D F L O O T T U

C E I O T W R W Y

Each of the words below can be turned into another word on the list by changing one letter and then rearranging them all to form a new word. For example, REGIMENT can be turned into STEERING by changing the M to an S, so they would be a pair. How quickly can you find all the pairs?

1. E B O N Y
2. G R O I N
3. U N T I L
4. B I N G O
5. D I T C H
6. B U I L T
7. B E A N O
8. C I T E D

Pairs

___ ___

___ ___

___ ___

___ ___

BANANA CRUNCH

LEVEL

Each set of ten tiles contains two common five-letter words. The letters of the first five-letter word are adjacent, but not in order. Find them and rearrange them to spell a word. Cross out those letters and rearrange the five remaining letters to spell the second word.

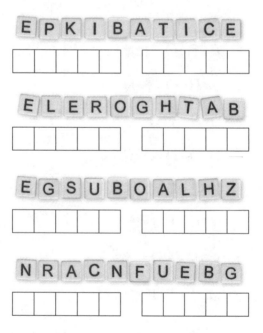

E P K I B A T I C E

E L E R O G H T A B

E G S U B O A L H Z

N R A C N F U E B G

Rearrange the letters of each word below and place them in the blanks so that, together with the two letters that have already been placed, they form a new word.

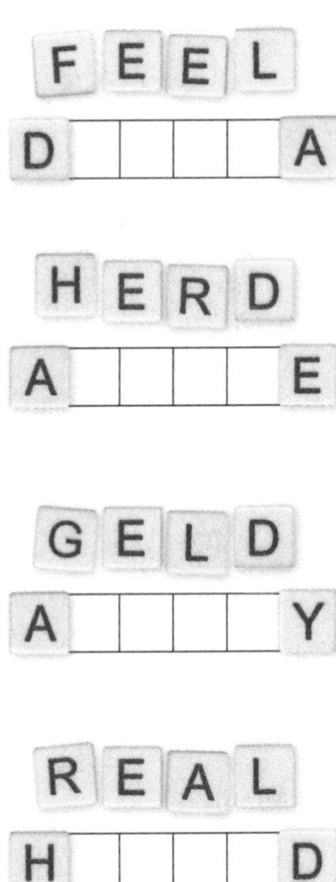

Use the 15 tiles in this bunch to create words that fit into the grids below. To get you started, a few tiles from the bunch have been placed in the grid. The BANANA BITES provide hints for one word to help you solve each grid. Reuse the 15 tiles in the bunch for each grid.

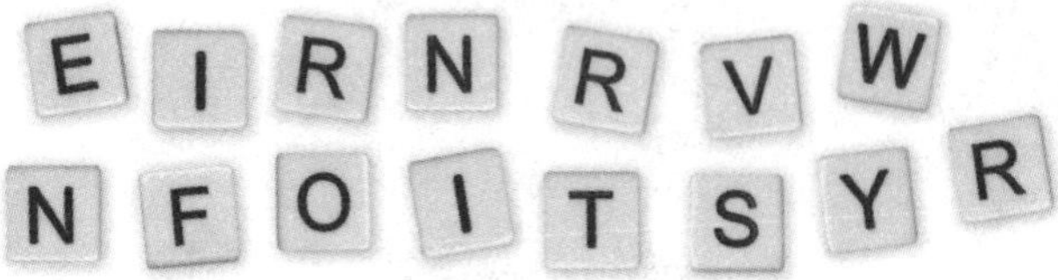

E I R N R V W
N F O I T S Y R

1. **BANANA BITE:**
A duplicate

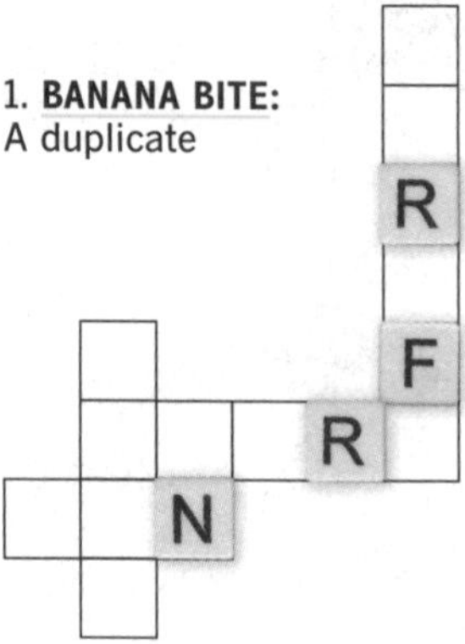

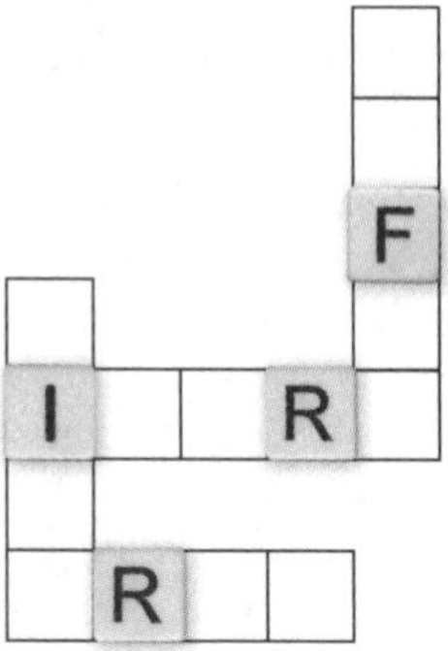

2. **BANANA BITE:**
Cool!

LEVEL

Each of the following six-letter sets can be rearranged to spell out a common word that either starts with IM, KN, or LA <u>or</u> ends with ED, IC, or LD. Find all the words as quickly as you can.

A C E L K Y

Add an R to each of the words below and then rearrange the letters in each word to form a new six-letter word.

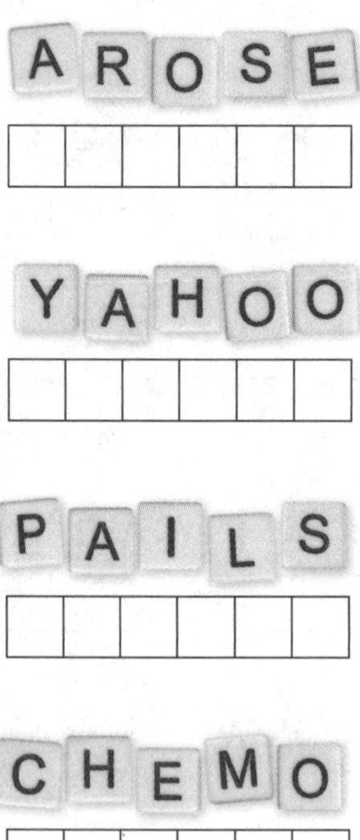

Each of the two-letter groups below may be extended on both the right and the left to form a six-letter word. Drawing from the tiles directly above each group, fill in the blanks to find the words as quickly as you can.

In each puzzle, use three of the tiles from the bunch to fill in the blanks and make a six-letter word that connects the grid.

Each set of letters is arranged alphabetically. The ? is in the correct alphabetical position. Figure out what letter the ? represents and rearrange the letters to spell a six-letter word that begins with the given letter. For example, in A?ENTV the ? could be an A, B, C, D, or E. Here it represents a D, which can be combined with the other letters to spell ADVENT.

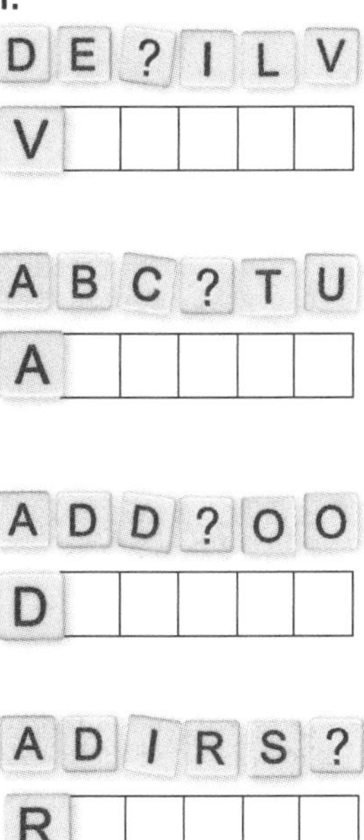

BANANA PEELS

LEVEL

There is one letter that when added to all of the four-letter words below can be used to form new five-letter words. Find the letter that works for all four words, add it to each word, and then rearrange each set of letters to form a new word. For example, B can be added to LOSS, ONLY, AUTO, and IRON to form SLOBS, NOBLY, ABOUT, and ROBIN.

COMMON LETTER

OMIT

HILT

DIET

SOLD

TOTALLY BANANAS

For each of the words below, replace one letter with the tile after the plus sign. Then rearrange the letters to spell something that is often sharp.

D O G E A R + G

L E A D E N + E

R O A D S + W

T O E I N G + U

Rearrange the tiles below to spell a five-letter word that fits in the first row. Then drop one letter and rearrange the remaining tiles to spell a four-letter word in the next row. Continue dropping one letter until you complete all four words. To get you started, one tile has been placed in each row.

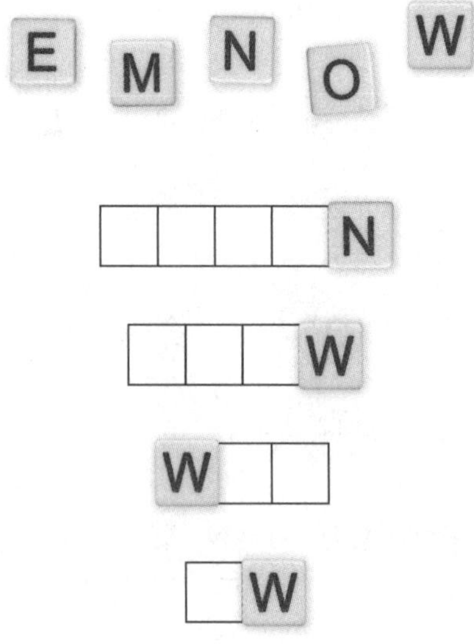

Using each two- and three-letter word just once, combine a word in the left column with a word in the right column. Then rearrange each five-letter scramble to form a word that begins with an A, T, or F and write it into the appropriate space below.

TI	FIT
HM	MAD
HA	BUT

A _ _ _ _

T _ _ _ _

F _ _ _ _

For each of the word groups below, change one letter in the top word to one of the letters that appears in the bottom word, then rearrange the tiles to form a new common word. Do the same with each new word until you arrive at the bottom word.

For example, one path from BARK to PLUM is BARK, MARK, RAMP, RUMP, PLUM.

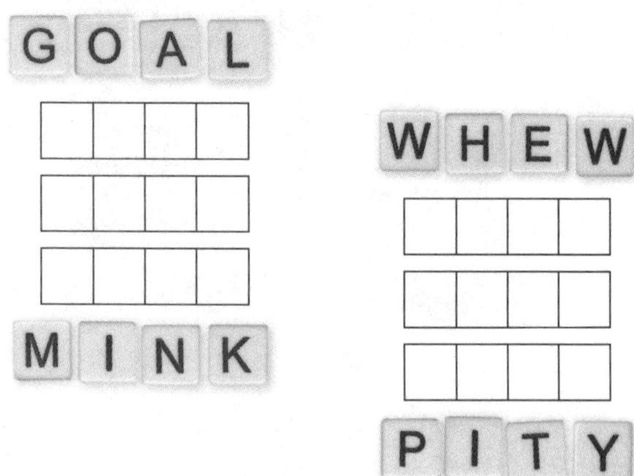

BUNCH OF BANANAS

LEVEL

For each word or phrase below, rearrange the letters to spell two one-word movie titles. For example, RACY WOKS can be rearranged to spell ROCKY, SAW. The first letter of each word is placed to get you started.

HOLY IN SPACE

A _ _ _ _ P _ _ _ _ _

A SHORT LILAC

L _ _ _ _ _ C _ _ _ _

LOVE SO RIGHT

G _ _ _ _ O _ _ _ _ _

IN FACT I MATE

T _ _ _ _ _ _ F _ _ _

For each bunch below, rearrange the letters to form two intersecting words that fit into the corresponding grid.

Each of the words below can be turned into another word on the list by changing one letter and then rearranging them all to form a new word. For example, REGIMENT can be turned into STEERING by changing the M to an S, so they would be a pair. How quickly can you find all the pairs?

1. FORCE
2. COLIC
3. TRUCK
4. MINUS
5. DECOR
6. OLEIC
7. MUSIC
8. COURT

Pairs

____ ____

____ ____

____ ____

____ ____

LEVEL

Each set of ten tiles contains two common five-letter words. The letters of the first five-letter word are adjacent, but not in order. Find them and rearrange them to spell a word. Cross out those letters and rearrange the five remaining letters to spell the second word.

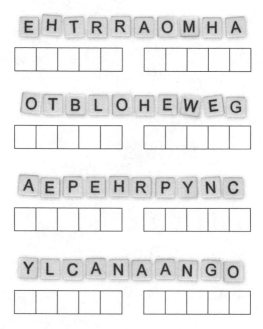

E H T R R A O M H A

O T B L O H E W E G

A E P E H R P Y N C

Y L C A N A A N G O

Rearrange the letters of each word below and place them in the blanks so that, together with the two letters that have already been placed, they form a new word.

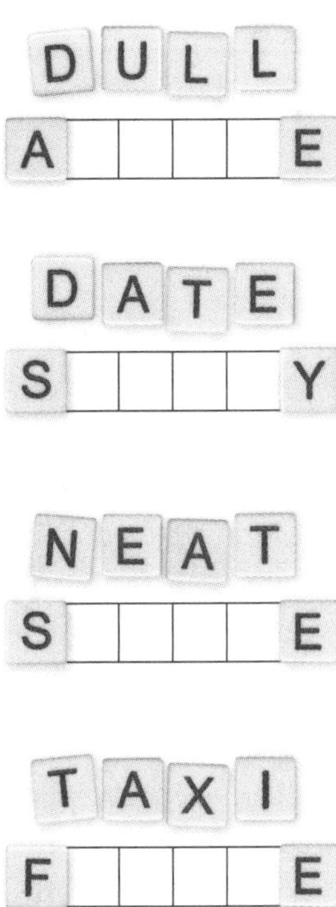

Use the 15 tiles in this bunch to create words that fit into the grids below. To get you started, a few tiles from the bunch have been placed in the grid. The BANANA BITES provide hints for one word to help you solve each grid. Reuse the 15 tiles in the bunch for each grid.

A E D T U V E
C F O A E X U Z

V D T O C

1. **BANANA BITE:** Long-standing fight

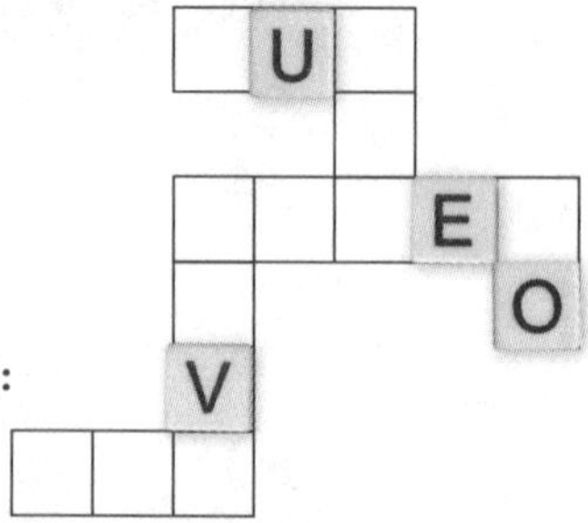

U E O V

2. **BANANA BITE:** Wedding suit

LEVEL

Each of the following six-letter sets can be rearranged to spell out a common word that either starts with FL, FR, or MI and/or ends with ER, ID, or RD. Find all the words as quickly as you can.

A E G H R T

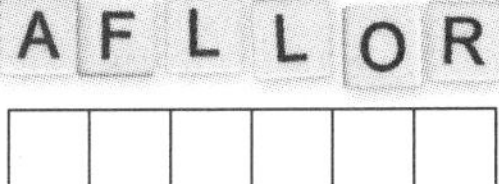

A B D R S U

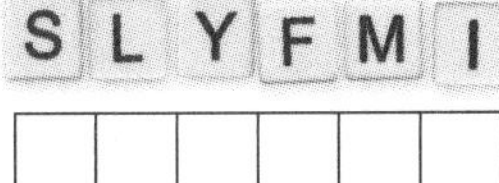

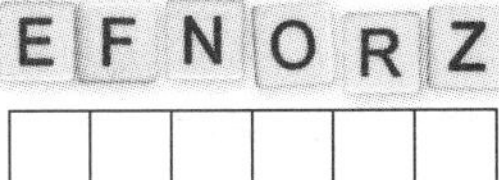

LEVEL

Add a C to each of the words below and then rearrange the letters in each word to form a new six-letter word.

BANANA PUDDING

Each of the two-letter groups below may be extended on both the right and the left to form a six-letter word. Drawing from the tiles directly above each group, fill in the blanks to find the words as quickly as you can.

In each puzzle, use three of the tiles from the bunch to fill in the blanks and make a six-letter word that connects the grid.

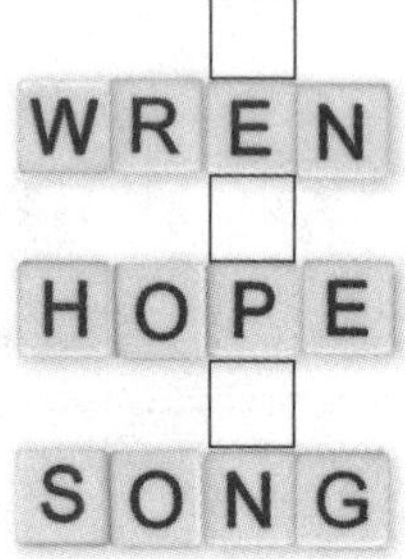

Each set of letters is arranged alphabetically. The ? is in the correct alphabetical position. Figure out what letter the ? represents and rearrange the letters to spell a six-letter word that begins with the given letter. For example, in A?ENTV the ? could be an A, B, C, D, or E. Here it represents a D, which can be combined with the other letters to spell ADVENT.

A B C E ? L

B _ _ _ _ _

A C D O R ?

C _ _ _ _ _

D E L M ? S

S _ _ _ _ _

A B G I ? T

G _ _ _ _ _

There is one letter that when added to all of the four-letter words below can be used to form new five-letter words. Find the letter that works for all four words, add it to each word, and then rearrange each set of letters to form a new word. For example, B can be added to LOSS, ONLY, AUTO, and IRON to form SLOBS, NOBLY, ABOUT, and ROBIN.

COMMON LETTER

☐

L I M P

☐☐☐☐☐

O M E N

☐☐☐☐☐

F O R E

☐☐☐☐☐

B A M S

☐☐☐☐☐

For each of the words below, replace one letter with the tile after the plus sign. Then rearrange the letters to spell something usually found in an airport.

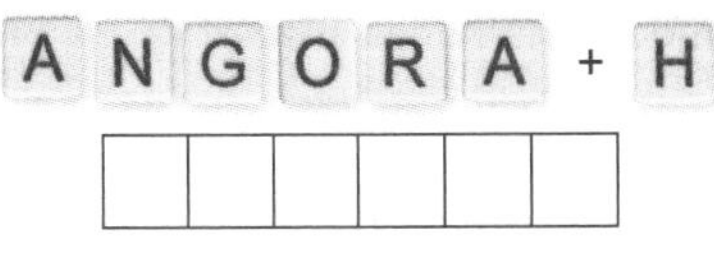

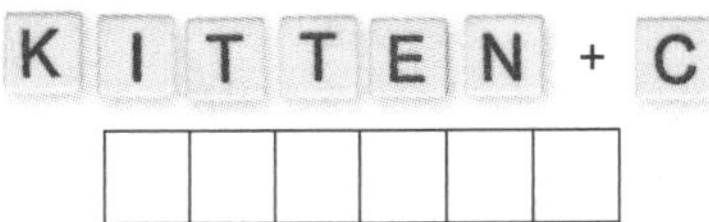

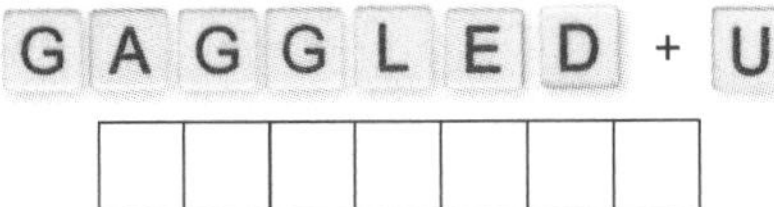

Rearrange the tiles below to spell a five-letter word that fits in the first row. Then drop one letter and rearrange the remaining tiles to spell a four-letter word in the next row. Continue dropping one letter until you complete all four words. To get you started, one tile has been placed in each row.

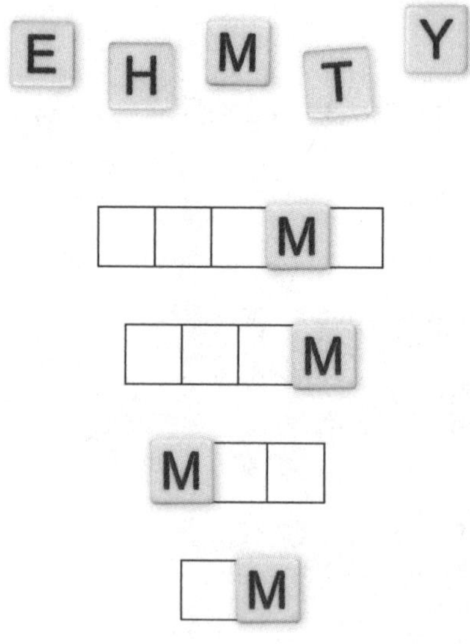

Using each two- and three-letter word just once, combine a word in the left column with a word in the right column. Then rearrange each five-letter scramble to form a word that begins with an H, L, or B and write it into the appropriate space below.

HA ROB

AN ILL

BE THE

H

L

B

For each of the word groups below, change one letter in the top word to one of the letters that appears in the bottom word, then rearrange the tiles to form a new common word. Do the same with each new word until you arrive at the bottom word.

For example, one path from BARK to PLUM is BARK, MARK, RAMP, RUMP, PLUM.

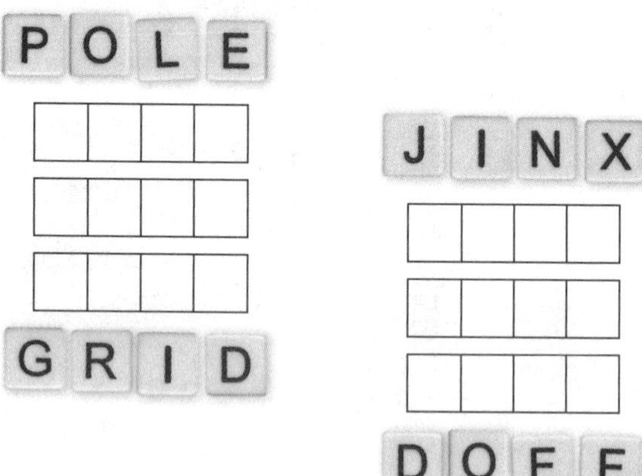

BUNCH OF BANANAS

For each word or phrase below, rearrange the letters to spell the last or only name of two famous fictional characters. For example, HOT MALE JERK can be rearranged to spell HAMLET, JOKER. The first letter of each word is placed to get you started.

BROKEN MUON

M _ _ _ B _ _ _ _ _

SUPER HOT TOE

H _ _ _ _ P _ _ _ _ _

HULA SUNK PERM

H _ _ _ S _ _ _ _ _ _ _

PROD THY COOKS

S _ _ _ _ D _ _ _ _ _ _

For each bunch below, rearrange the letters to form two intersecting words that fit into the corresponding grid.

A A E E I N V V W

A B E M M M O O R

LEVEL

Each of the words below can be turned into another word on the list by changing one letter and then rearranging them all to form a new word. For example, REGIMENT can be turned into STEERING by changing the M to an S, so they would be a pair. How quickly can you find all the pairs?

1. SCORE
2. MIDST
3. DEIFY
4. STAID
5. ROUSE
6. 

7. DONUT
8. OUTDO

Pairs

___ ___

___ ___

___ ___

___ ___

Each set of ten tiles contains two common five-letter words. The letters of the first five-letter word are adjacent, but not in order. Find them and rearrange them to spell a word. Cross out those letters and rearrange the five remaining letters to spell the second word.

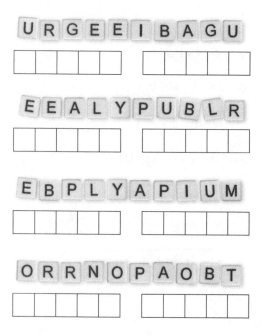

U R G E E I B A G U

E E A L Y P U B L R

E B P L Y A P I U M

O R R N O P A O B T

Rearrange the letters of each word below and place them in the blanks so that, together with the two letters that have already been placed, they form a new word.

Use the 15 tiles in this bunch to create words that fit into the grids below. To get you started, a few tiles from the bunch have been placed in the grid. The BANANA BITES provide hints for one word to help you solve each grid. Reuse the 15 tiles in the bunch for each grid.

A O R D P N T
K P H T O S W M

1. **BANANA BITE:** Made smaller

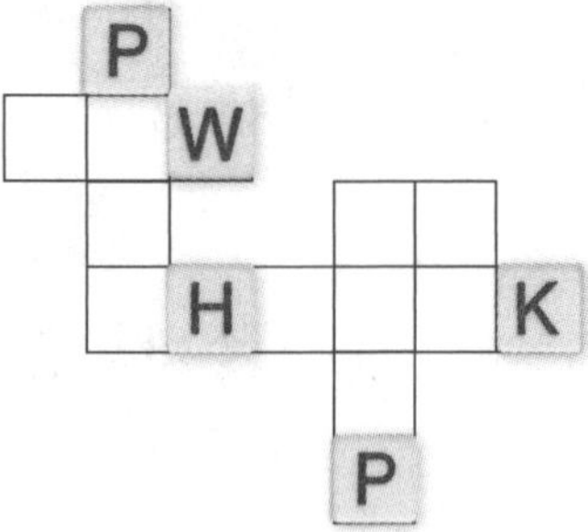

P W H K P

N D R M

2. **BANANA BITE:** Not tall

BANANA SHAKES

LEVEL

Each of the following six-letter sets can be rearranged to spell out a common word that either starts with NO, PL, or PR or ends with NT, RT, or ST. Find all the words as quickly as you can.

D E I R T V

E E R R T V

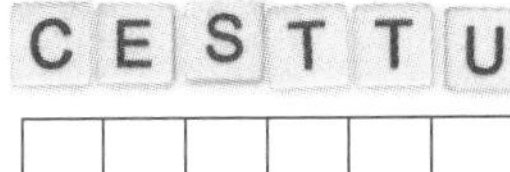

D E E G L P

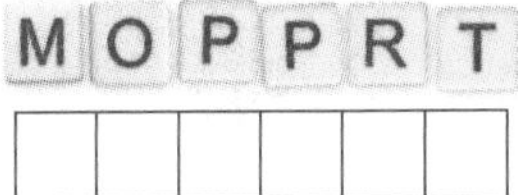

Add an M to each of the words below and then rearrange the letters in each word to form a new six-letter word.

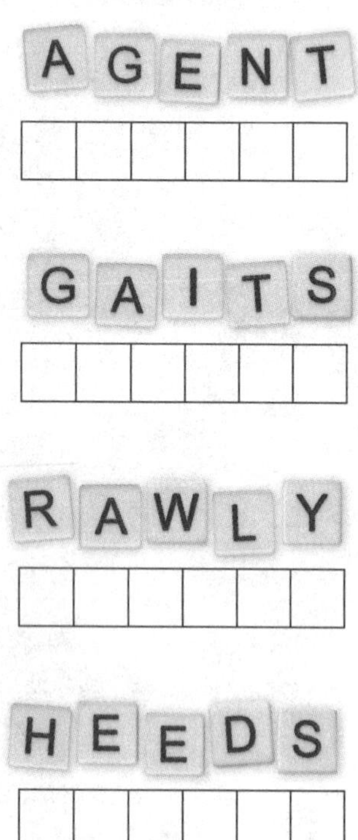

BANANA PUDDING

LEVEL

Each of the two-letter groups below may be extended on both the right and the left to form a six-letter word. Drawing from the tiles directly above each group, fill in the blanks to find the words as quickly as you can.

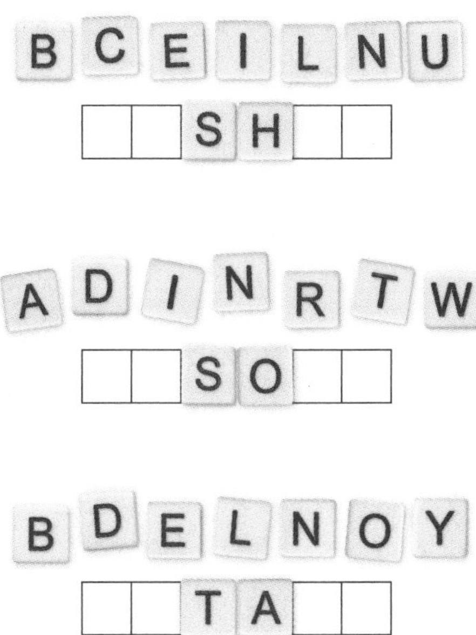

BANANA LEAVES

In each puzzle, use three of the tiles from the bunch to fill in the blanks and make a six-letter word that connects the grid.

B M F O R S U

GONE
BEAT
LEAP

DRANK
AREA
IDOL

F L I M O R T

Each set of letters is arranged alphabetically. The ? is in the correct alphabetical position. Figure out what letter the ? represents and rearrange the letters to spell a six-letter word that begins with the given letter. For example, in A?ENTV the ? could be an A, B, C, D, or E. Here it represents a D, which can be combined with the other letters to spell ADVENT.

There is one letter that when added to all of the four-letter words below can be used to form new five-letter words. Find the letter that works for all four words, add it to each word, and then rearrange each set of letters to form a new word. For example, B can be added to LOSS, ONLY, AUTO, and IRON to form SLOBS, NOBLY, ABOUT, and ROBIN.

COMMON LETTER

☐

Y O R E

☐☐☐☐☐

M I E N

☐☐☐☐☐

W H E N

☐☐☐☐☐

Y I P S

☐☐☐☐☐

For each of the words below, replace one letter with the tile after the plus sign. Then rearrange the letters to spell a number.

H O G T I E + Y

D E N S E + V

E A T E R + H

Rearrange the tiles below to spell a five-letter word that fits in the first row. Then drop one letter and rearrange the remaining tiles to spell a four-letter word in the next row. Continue dropping one letter until you complete all four words. To get you started, one tile has been placed in each row.

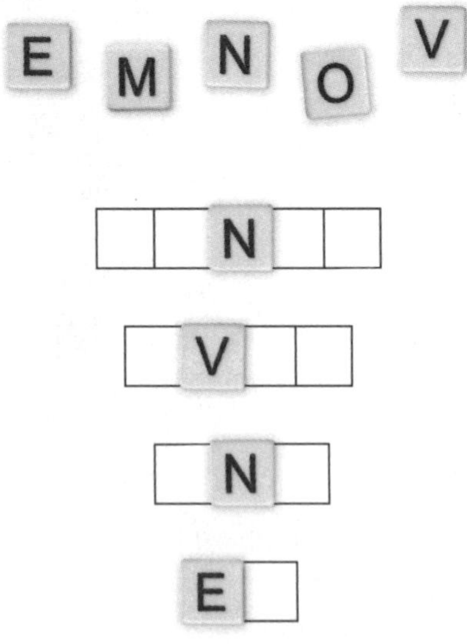

Using each two- and three-letter word just once, combine a word in the left column with a word in the right column. Then rearrange each five-letter scramble to form a word that begins with a B, G, or H and write it into the appropriate space below.

GO	VEG
LA	AUK
HI	HUB

B

G

H

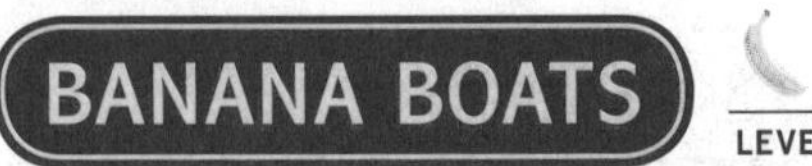

For each of the word groups below, change one letter in the top word to one of the letters that appears in the bottom word, then rearrange the tiles to form a new common word. Do the same with each new word until you arrive at the bottom word.

For example, one path from BARK to PLUM is BARK, MARK, RAMP, RUMP, PLUM.

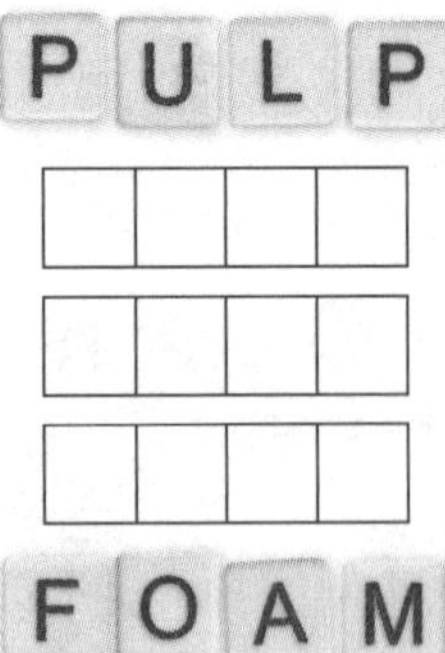

BUNCH OF BANANAS

For each word or phrase below, rearrange the letters to spell two things that each can form a compound word when TIME is added to its end. For example, DRAW MARE can be rearranged to spell DREAMtime, WARtime. The first letter of each word is placed to get you started.

WHOSE CAPE

P _ _ _ _ S _ _ _

GREMLIN SAP

S _ _ _ _ _ M _ _ _

FRIED LINEN

D _ _ _ _ _ L _ _ _

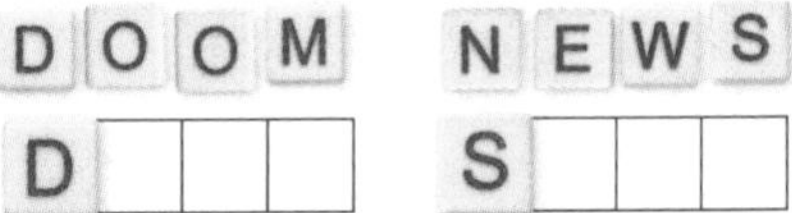

For each bunch below, rearrange the letters to form two intersecting words that fit into the corresponding grid.

B E E E E G I N T

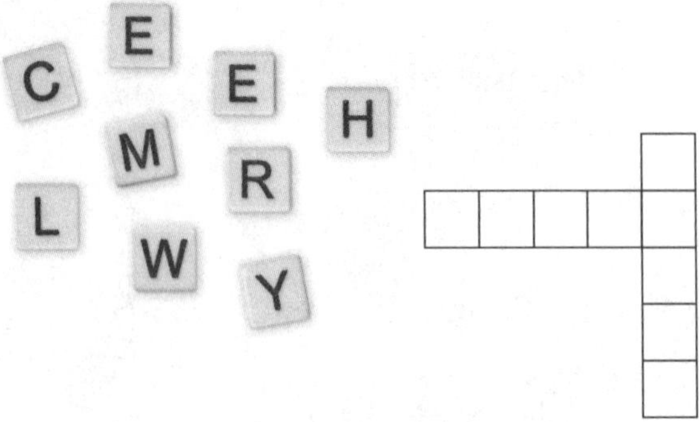

C E E H M R L W Y

Each of the words below can be turned into another word on the list by changing one letter and then rearranging them all to form a new word. For example, REGIMENT can be turned into STEERING by changing the M to an S, so they would be a pair. How quickly can you find all the pairs?

1. COUNT
2. PARTY
3. DOWEL
4. PEKOE
5. PUTON
6. CRYPT
7. WOULD
8. ELOPE

Pairs

___ ___

___ ___

___ ___

___ ___

BANANA CRUNCH

LEVEL

Each set of ten tiles contains two common five-letter words. The letters of the first five-letter word are adjacent, but not in order. Find them and rearrange them to spell a word. Cross out those letters and rearrange the five remaining letters to spell the second word.

T F E M A W N O B I

U F O D L N B C O S

Y R U I O T A R V C

O O Y M C F N O I N

Rearrange the letters of each word below and place them in the blanks so that, together with the two letters that have already been placed, they form a new word.

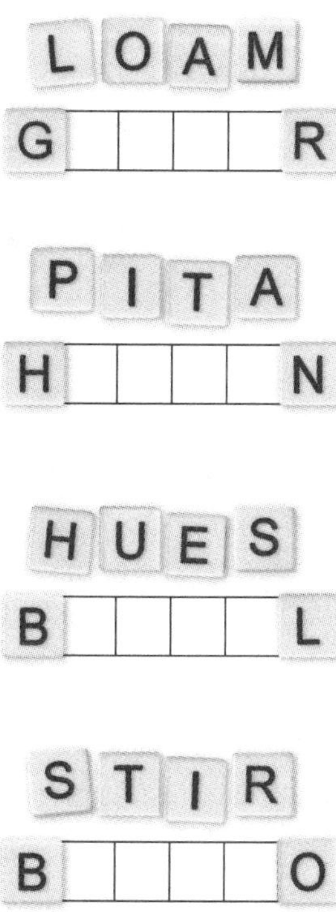

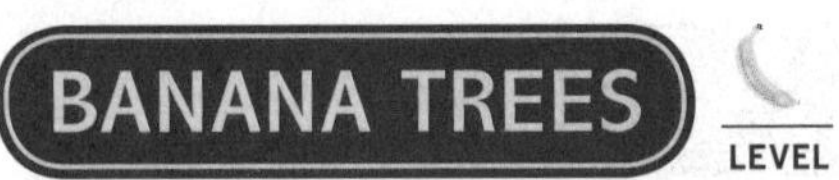

Use the 15 tiles in this bunch to create words that fit into the grids below. To get you started, a few tiles from the bunch have been placed in the grid. The BANANA BITES provide hints for one word to help you solve each grid. Reuse the 15 tiles in the bunch for each grid.

C E A L E U I

A J I D N Q E L

E

N

I I

1. **BANANA BITE:** Place for outlaws

A

I U

E

L

2. **BANANA BITE:** Precious stone

Each of the following six-letter sets can be rearranged to spell out a common word that either starts with RE, SP, or ST and/or ends with CE, DE, or OR. Find all the words as quickly as you can.

A L L O P R

C E O R R T

A D E M N U

A E E K M R

A C D E E F

C E I L P S

Add an H to each of the words below and then rearrange the letters in each word to form a new six-letter word.

BANANA PUDDING

Each of the two-letter groups below may be extended on both the right and the left to form a six-letter word. Drawing from the tiles directly above each group, fill in the blanks to find the words as quickly as you can.

In each puzzle, use three of the tiles from the bunch to fill in the blanks and make a six-letter word that connects the grid.

A C B E O P T

WRAP
HYPE
ANTE

BROWN
CLUE
TREAT

A G B I L R T

Each set of letters is arranged alphabetically. The ? is in the correct alphabetical position. Figure out what letter the ? represents and rearrange the letters to spell a six-letter word that begins with the given letter. For example, in A?ENTV the ? could be an A, B, C, D, or E. Here it represents a D, which can be combined with the other letters to spell ADVENT.

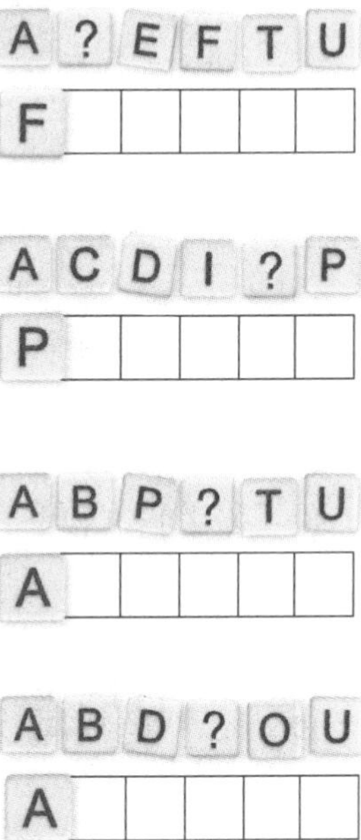

There is one letter that when added to all of the four-letter words below can be used to form new five-letter words. Find the letter that works for all four words, add it to each word, and then rearrange each set of letters to form a new word. For example, B can be added to LOSS, ONLY, AUTO, and IRON to form SLOBS, NOBLY, ABOUT, and ROBIN.

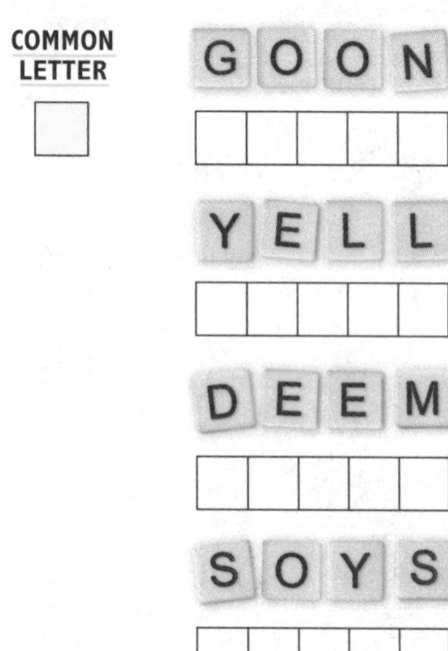

TOTALLY BANANAS

For each of the words below, replace one letter with the tile after the plus sign. Then rearrange the letters to spell something found in restaurants.

T U N E + M

S I D E + H

R O B O T + H

C E N T E R + E

Rearrange the tiles below to spell a five-letter word that fits in the first row. Then drop one letter and rearrange the remaining tiles to spell a four-letter word in the next row. Continue dropping one letter until you complete all four words. To get you started, one tile has been placed in each row.

Using each two- and three-letter word just once, combine a word in the left column with a word in the right column. Then rearrange each five-letter scramble to form a word that begins with an M, A, or L and write it into the appropriate space below.

N O	P A D
T O	M U D
A H	L U G

M _ _ _ _

A _ _ _ _

L _ _ _ _

For the word group below, change one letter in the top word to one of the letters that appears in the bottom word, then rearrange the tiles to form a new common word. Do the same with each new word until you arrive at the bottom word.

For example, one path from BARK to PLUM is BARK, MARK, RAMP, RUMP, PLUM.

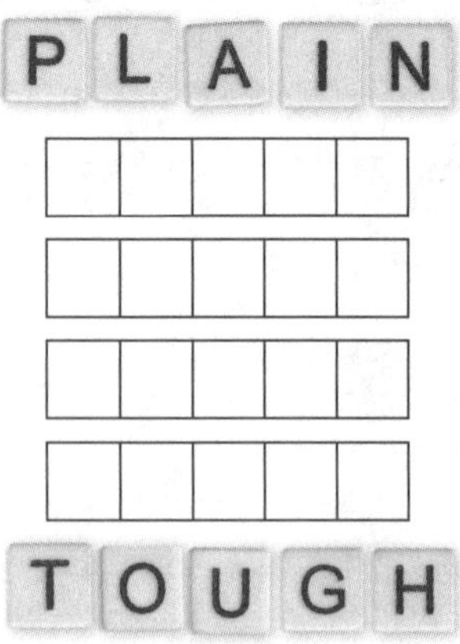

BUNCH OF BANANAS

For each word or phrase below, rearrange the letters to spell two things that are gems, stones, or rocks. For example, PEAR SHAPE BRIM can be rearranged to spell SAPPHIRE, AMBER. The first letter of one word is placed to get you started.

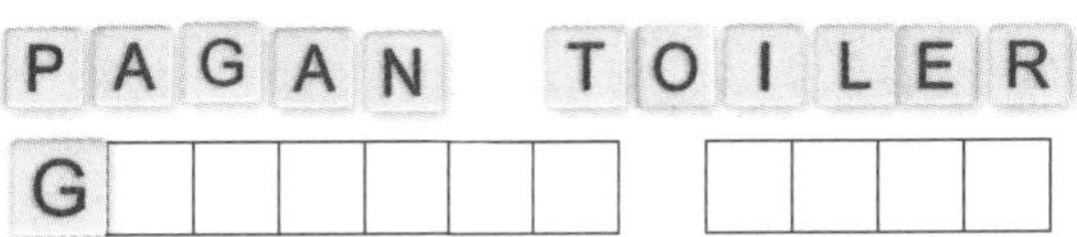

For each bunch below, rearrange the letters to form two intersecting words that fit into the corresponding grid.

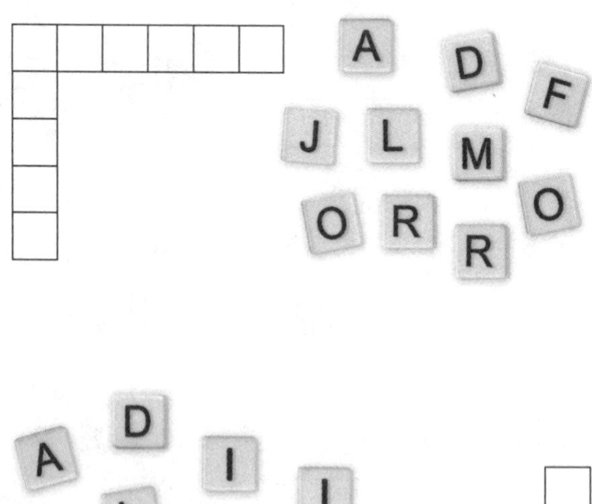

A D I I
L L O
U P V

Each of the words below can be turned into another word on the list by changing one letter and then rearranging them all to form a new word. For example, REGIMENT can be turned into STEERING by changing the M to an S, so they would be a pair. How quickly can you find all the pairs?

1. CARAFE
2. ADAGIO
3. OBTAIN
4. ARCANE
5. BRUTAL
6. BANDIT
7. PAGODA
8. TABULI

Pairs

___ ___

___ ___

___ ___

___ ___

LEVEL

Each set of 11 tiles contains one common five-letter word and one common six-letter word. The letters of the five-letter word are adjacent, but not in order. Find them and rearrange them to spell a word. Cross out those letters and rearrange the six remaining letters to spell the second word.

N N A N E X Y S H A E

R G G Y A V R N G O O

P T O K A H N T I T P

T J U A I L T V N U S

BANANA BITES

LEVEL

Rearrange the letters of each word below and place them in the blanks so that, together with the two letters that have already been placed, they form a new word.

Use the 15 tiles in this bunch to create words that fit into the grids below. To get you started, a few tiles from the bunch have been placed in the grid. The BANANA BITES provide hints for one word to help you solve each grid. Reuse the 15 tiles in the bunch for each grid.

1. **BANANA BITE:**
Mixes thoroughly

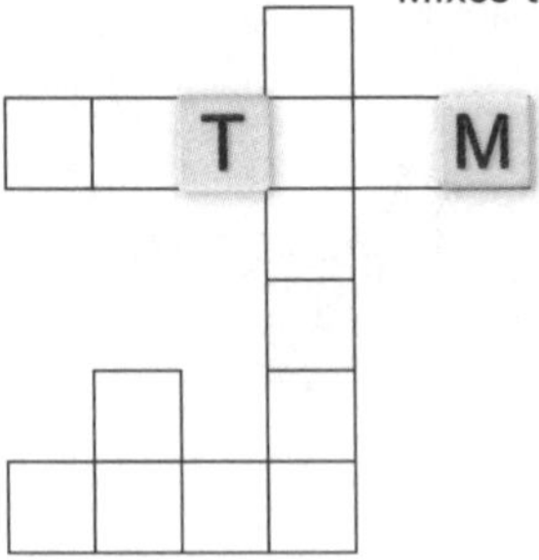

T M

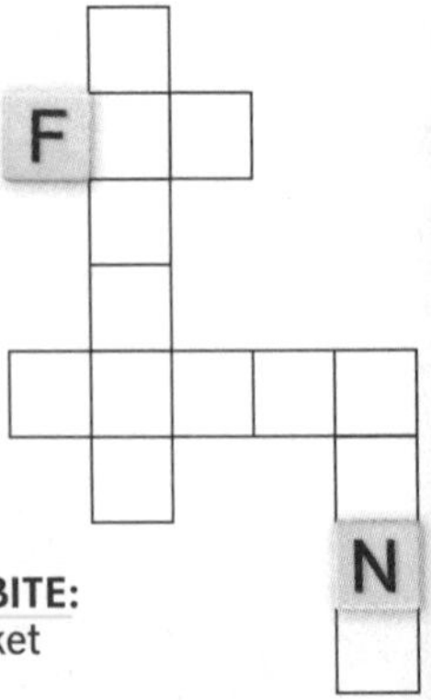

F

N

2. **BANANA BITE:**
Animal pocket

LEVEL

Each of the following six-letter sets can be rearranged to spell out a common word that either starts with C, B, or R and/or ends with N, D, or T. Find all the words as quickly as you can.

A C D D I N

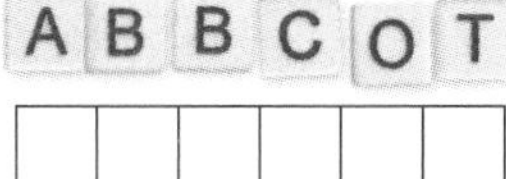

A D E G K W

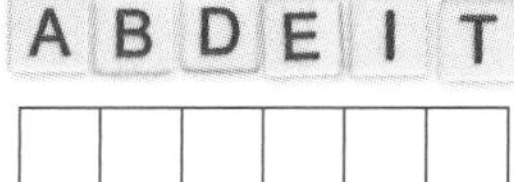

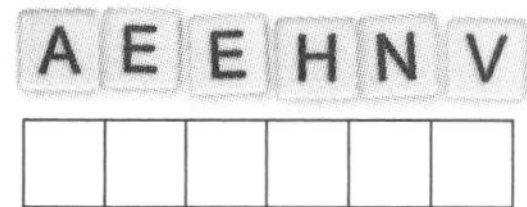

LEVEL

Add a D to each of the words below and then rearrange the letters in each word to form a new seven-letter word.

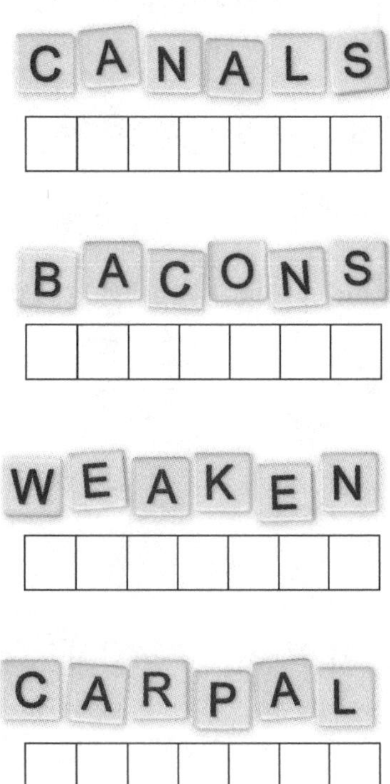

Each of the three-letter groups below may be extended on both the right and the left to form a seven-letter word. Drawing from the tiles directly above each group, fill in the blanks to find the words as quickly as you can.

LEVEL

In each puzzle, use four of the tiles from the bunch to fill in the blanks and make a seven-letter word that connects the grid.

A E C P T W Y

GRATE
THAT
MART

SCUD
OUR
FROG

A N A O S T Y

Each set of letters is arranged alphabetically. The ? is in the correct alphabetical position. Figure out what letter the ? represents and rearrange the letters to spell a six-letter word that ends with the given letter. For example, in A?ENTV the ? could be an A, B, C, D, or E. Here it represents a D, which can be combined with the other letters to spell ADVENT.

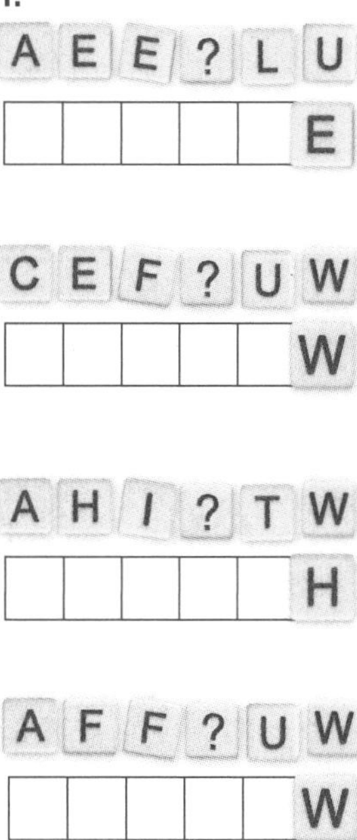

There is one letter that when added to all of the five-letter words below can be used to form new six-letter words. Find the letter that works for all four words, add it to each word, and then rearrange each set of letters to form a new word. For example, B can be added to LOSS, ONLY, AUTO, and IRON to form SLOBS, NOBLY, ABOUT, and ROBIN.

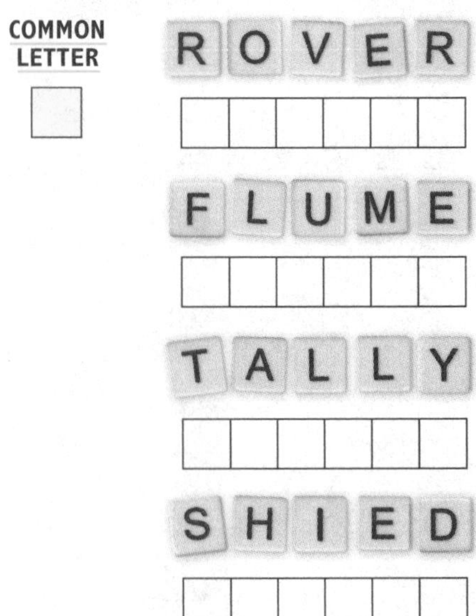

LEVEL

For each of the words below, replace one letter with the tile after the plus sign. Then rearrange the letters to spell something typically found in bathrooms.

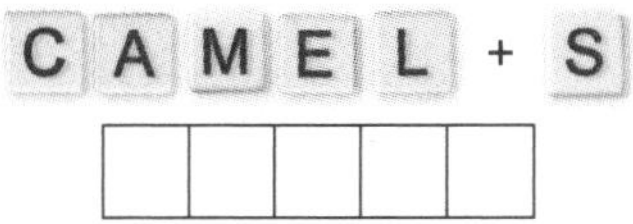

O T H E R S + W

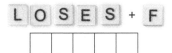

L O S E S + F

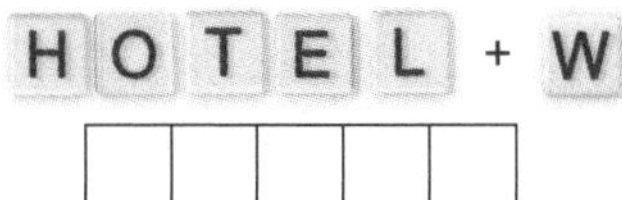

Rearrange the tiles below to spell a six-letter word that fits in the first row. Then drop one letter and rearrange the remaining tiles to spell a five-letter word in the next row. Continue dropping one letter until you complete all five words. To get you started, one tile has been placed in each row.

A A I N T T

					N

		T		

		N	

N		

	N

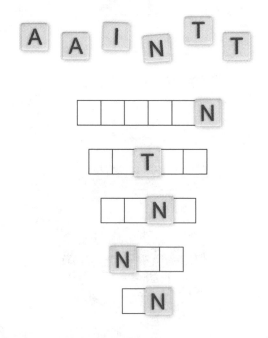

LEVEL

Using each three-letter word just once, combine a word in the left column with a word in the right column. Then rearrange each six-letter scramble to form a word that begins with a B or C and write it into the appropriate space below.

M A D	S A C
A C E	N A B
V A N	R A M

B _ _ _ _ _

C _ _ _ _ _

C _ _ _ _ _

For the word group below, change one letter in the top word to one of the letters that appears in the bottom word, then rearrange the tiles to form a new common word. Do the same with each new word until you arrive at the bottom word.

For example, one path from BARK to PLUM is BARK, MARK, RAMP, RUMP, PLUM.

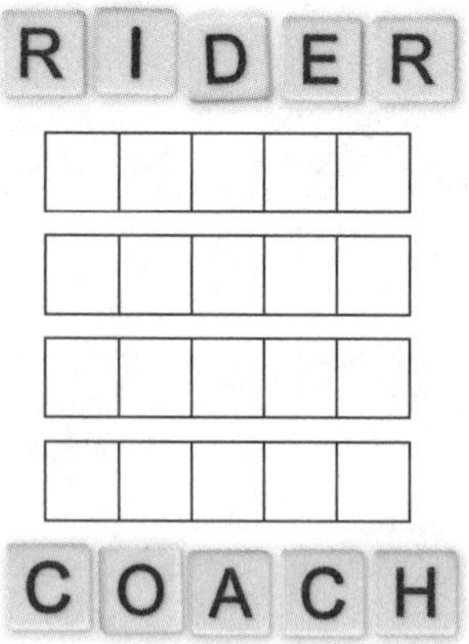

BUNCH OF BANANAS

LEVEL

For each word or phrase below, rearrange the letters to spell two last (or only) names of singers. For example, SENOR IMBIBE can be rearranged to spell Justin BIEBER, Paul SIMON. The first letter of one word is placed to get you started.

A DRESSY PLAN

S _ _ _ _ _   _ _ _ _ _

MEGA ENIGMA

G _ _ _   _ _ _ _ _ _

SPIN YODELER

P _ _ _ _ _ _   _ _ _ _

A RICH NEWT

C _ _ _   _ _ _ _ _

For each bunch below, rearrange the letters to form two intersecting words that fit into the corresponding grid.

A A D M M N T Y Z O

A C C D I N D U S U

Each of the words below can be turned into another word on the list by changing one letter and then rearranging them all to form a new word. For example, REGIMENT can be turned into STEERING by changing the M to an S, so they would be a pair. How quickly can you find all the pairs?

1. CALICO
2. ATONED
3. SEANCE
4. DEACON
5. SOCIAL
6. CHANGE
7. UNEASE
8. AGENCY

Pairs

___ ___

___ ___

___ ___

___ ___

Each set of 11 tiles contains one common five-letter word and one common six-letter word. The letters of the five-letter word are adjacent, but not in order. Find them and rearrange them to spell a word. Cross out those letters and rearrange the six remaining letters to spell the second word.

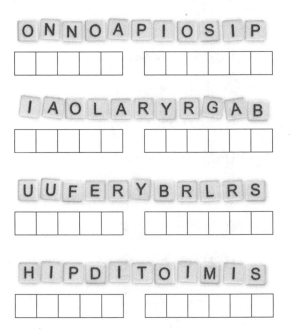

O N N O A P I O S I P

I A O L A R Y R G A B

U U F E R Y B R L R S

H I P D I T O I M I S

Rearrange the letters of each word below and place them in the blanks so that, together with the two letters that have already been placed, they form a new word.

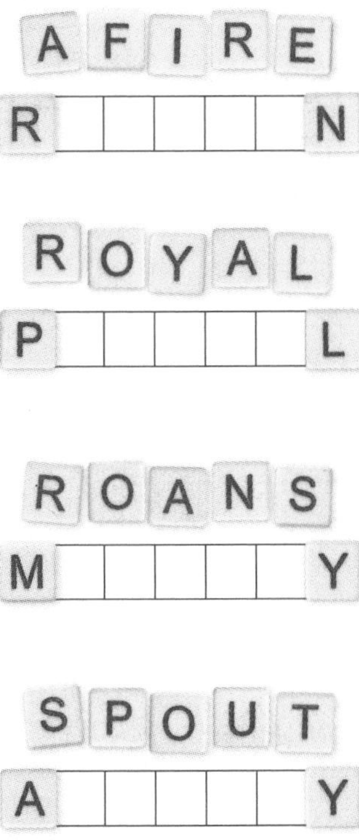

Use the 15 tiles in this bunch to create words that fit into the grids below. To get you started, a few tiles from the bunch have been placed in the grid. The BANANA BITES provide hints for one word to help you solve each grid. Reuse the 15 tiles in the bunch for each grid.

D P H O I M R
I E M I T U T V

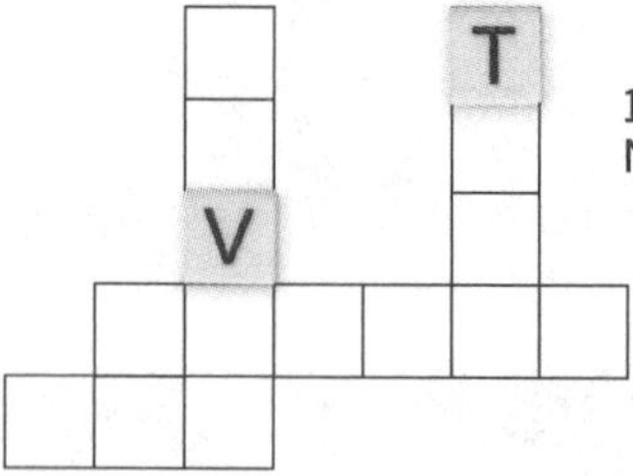

T
V

1. **BANANA BITE:**
Not large or small

M
O

2. **BANANA BITE:**
Good trait

Each of the following six-letter sets can be rearranged to spell out a common word that either starts with D, E, or I and/or ends with D, R, or S. Find all the words as quickly as you can.

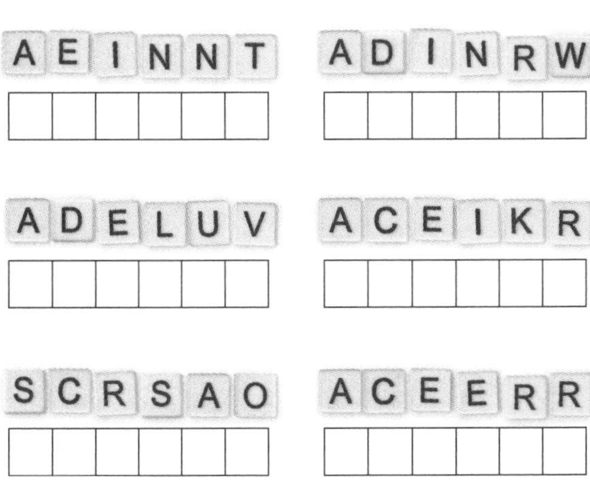

Add a G to each of the words below and then rearrange the letters in each word to form a new seven-letter word.

Each of the three-letter groups below may be extended on both the right and the left to form a seven-letter word. Drawing from the tiles directly above each group, fill in the blanks to find the words as quickly as you can.

LEVEL

In each puzzle, use four of the tiles from the bunch to fill in the blanks and make a seven-letter word that connects the grid.

D N E R S T W

```
  _
N A M E
  _
T H U G
  _
Z A N Y
  _
```

```
    _
D E F Y
    _
B A B Y
    _
  M A R R Y
    _
```

A F E N O R T

Each set of letters is arranged alphabetically. The ? is in the correct alphabetical position. Figure out what letter the ? represents and rearrange the letters to spell a six-letter word that ends with the given letter. For example, in A?ENTV the ? could be an A, B, C, D, or E. Here it represents a D, which can be combined with the other letters to spell ADVENT.

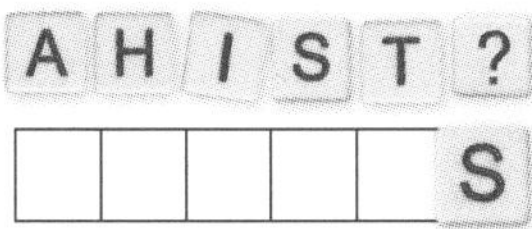

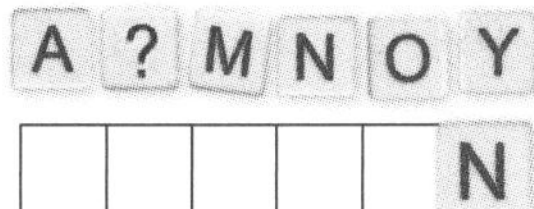

There is one letter that when added to all of the five-letter words below can be used to form new six-letter words. Find the letter that works for all four words, add it to each word, and then rearrange each set of letters to form a new word. For example, B can be added to LOSS, ONLY, AUTO, and IRON to form SLOBS, NOBLY, ABOUT, and ROBIN.

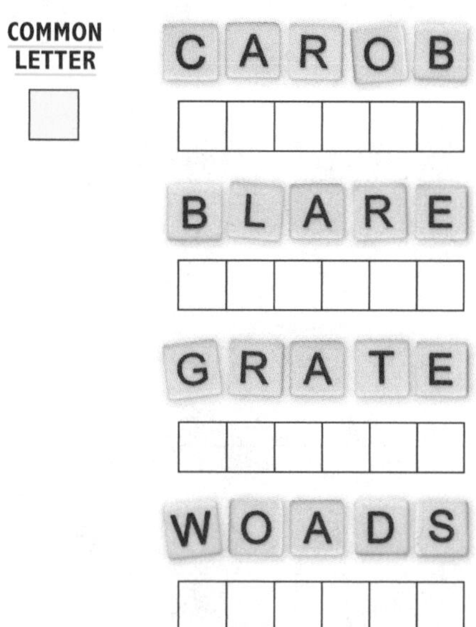

LEVEL

For each of the words below, replace one letter with the tile after the plus sign. Then rearrange the letters to spell a type of building.

S H O R E + U

☐☐☐☐☐

C H A P E L + A

☐☐☐☐☐☐

A L T E R S + B

☐☐☐☐☐☐

S E N I O R + P

☐☐☐☐☐☐

Rearrange the tiles below to spell a six-letter word that fits in the first row. Then drop one letter and rearrange the remaining tiles to spell a five-letter word in the next row. Continue dropping one letter until you complete all five words. To get you started, one tile has been placed in each row.

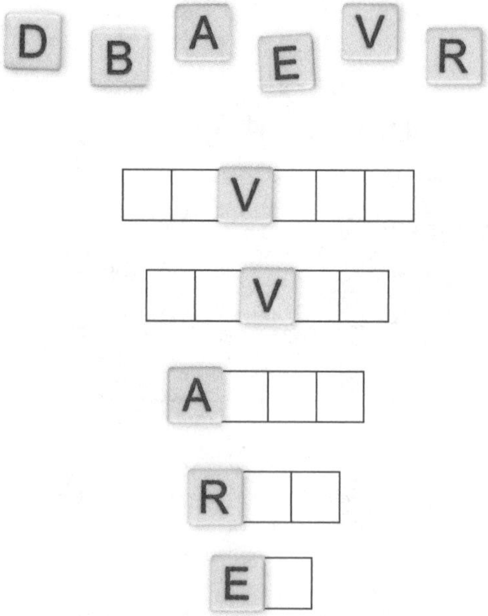

D B A E V R

		V			

		V		

A			

R		

E	

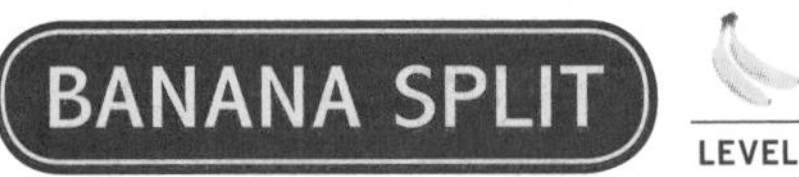

Using each three-letter word just once, combine a word in the left column with a word in the right column. Then rearrange each six-letter scramble to form a word that begins with an A, C, or G and write it into the appropriate space below.

C A R	A P E
G A G	E A R
P A R	N A Y

A _ _ _ _ _

C _ _ _ _ _

G _ _ _ _ _

For the word group below, change one letter in the top word to one of the letters that appears in the bottom word, then rearrange the tiles to form a new common word. Do the same with each new word until you arrive at the bottom word.

For example, one path from BARK to PLUM is BARK, MARK, RAMP, RUMP, PLUM.

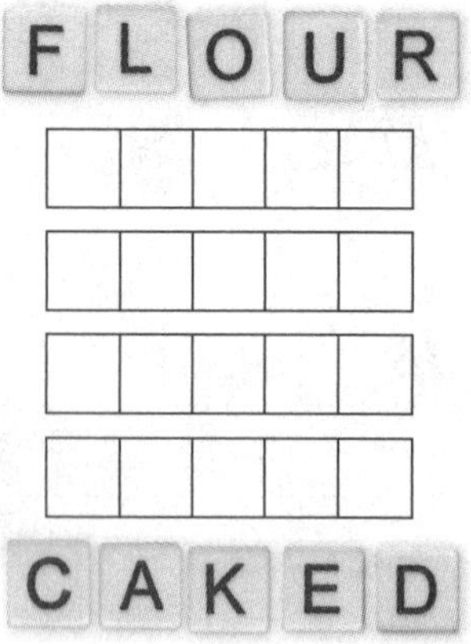

BUNCH OF BANANAS

For each word or phrase below, rearrange the letters to spell two animals. For example, REAL ECHO can be rearranged to spell ROACH, EEL. The first letter of one word is placed to get you started.

HER NOTEPAD

☐☐☐ P☐☐☐☐☐☐

HEART FLAMES

H☐☐☐☐☐☐ ☐☐☐☐

FRIGATE FAN

G☐☐☐☐☐☐ ☐☐☐

TERRAN SOCK

C☐☐☐☐ ☐☐☐☐☐

For each bunch below, rearrange the letters to form two intersecting words that fit into the corresponding grid.

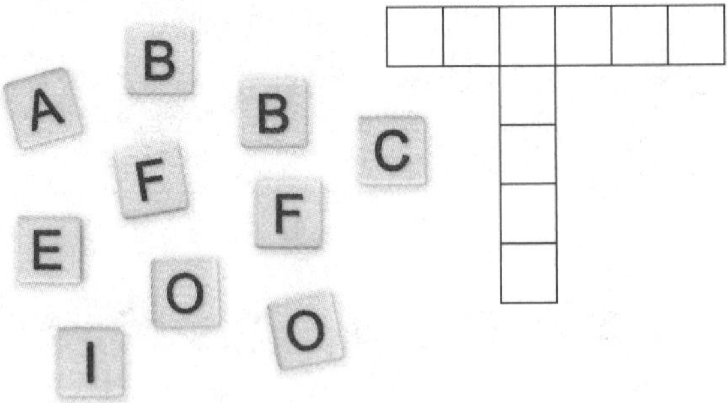

A C I I I L M S Y M

B A B C F E F O I O

Each of the words below can be turned into another word on the list by changing one letter and then rearranging them all to form a new word. For example, REGIMENT can be turned into STEERING by changing the M to an S, so they would be a pair. How quickly can you find all the pairs?

1. LAUNCH
2. SITCOM
3. ASLEEP
4. DANISH
5. MOSAIC
6. UNCLAD
7. EMPALE
8. ISLAND

Pairs

___ ___

___ ___

___ ___

___ ___

BANANA CRUNCH

LEVEL

Each set of 11 tiles contains one common five-letter word and one common six-letter word. The letters of the five-letter word are adjacent, but not in order. Find them and rearrange them to spell a word. Cross out those letters and rearrange the six remaining letters to spell the second word.

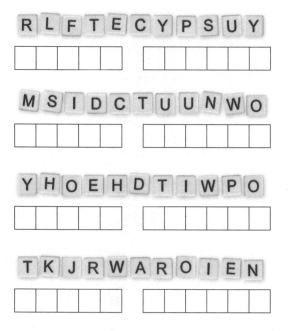

R L F T E C Y P S U Y

M S I D C T U U N W O

Y H O E H D T I W P O

T K J R W A R O I E N

Rearrange the letters of each word below and place them in the blanks so that, together with the two letters that have already been placed, they form a new word.

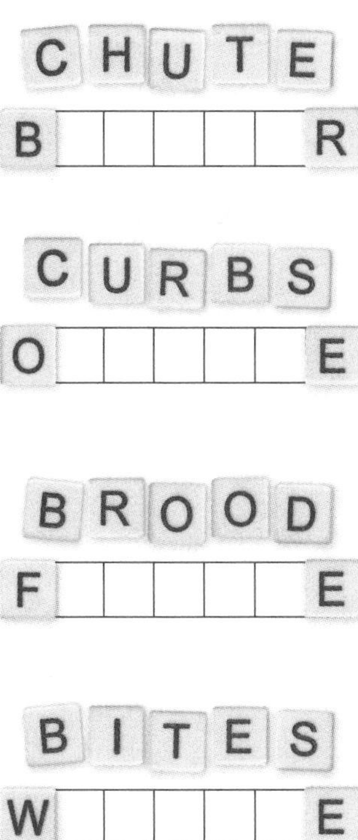

Use the 15 tiles in this bunch to create words that fit into the grids below. To get you started, a few tiles from the bunch have been placed in the grid. The BANANA BITES provide hints for one word to help you solve each grid. Reuse the 15 tiles in the bunch for each grid.

A K R I E I O

E D G O S E X E

1. **BANANA BITE:**
Oxygen compounds

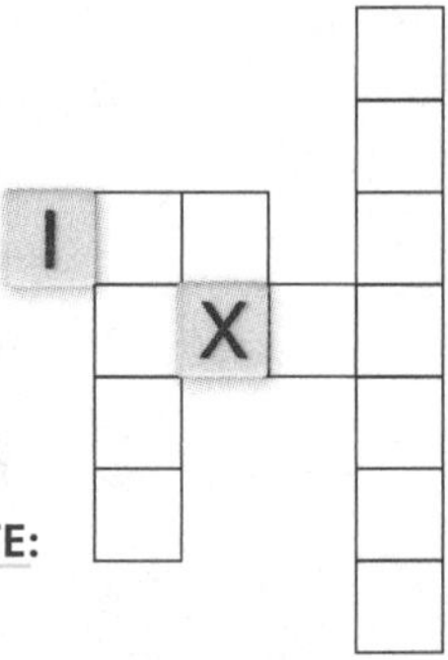

K

I

I X

2. **BANANA BITE:**
Bag of treats

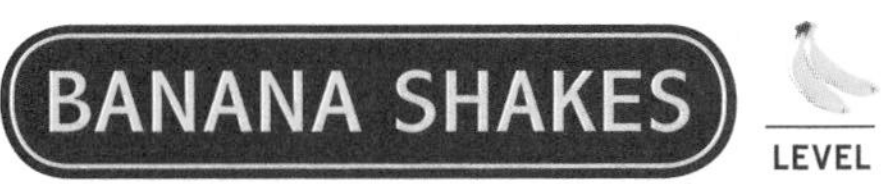

LEVEL

Each of the following six-letter sets can be rearranged to spell out a common word that either starts with F, H, or L <u>or</u> ends with A, L, or M. Find all the words as quickly as you can.

A E H M M Y

A A C L N O

A C E F T U

A C C E L N

A D I L R Z

B E E L M M

A H I L S V

A B H O R R

Add an L to each of the words below and then rearrange the letters in each word to form a new seven-letter word.

Each of the three-letter groups below may be extended on both the right and the left to form a seven-letter word. Drawing from the tiles directly above each group, fill in the blanks to find the words as quickly as you can.

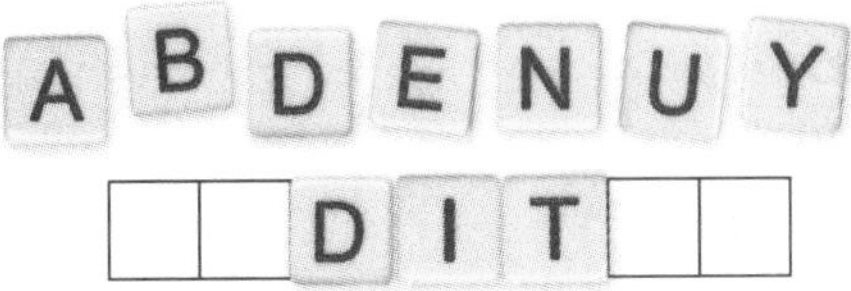

BANANA LEAVES

LEVEL

In each puzzle, use four of the tiles from the bunch to fill in the blanks and make a seven-letter word that connects the grid.

D L E M U R Y

CENT
HOLY
BEST

MELT
TUG
UNIT

E I G N P R T

Each set of letters is arranged alphabetically. The ? is in the correct alphabetical position. Figure out what letter the ? represents and rearrange the letters to spell a six-letter word that ends with the given letter. For example, in A?ENTV the ? could be an A, B, C, D, or E. Here it represents a D, which can be combined with the other letters to spell ADVENT.

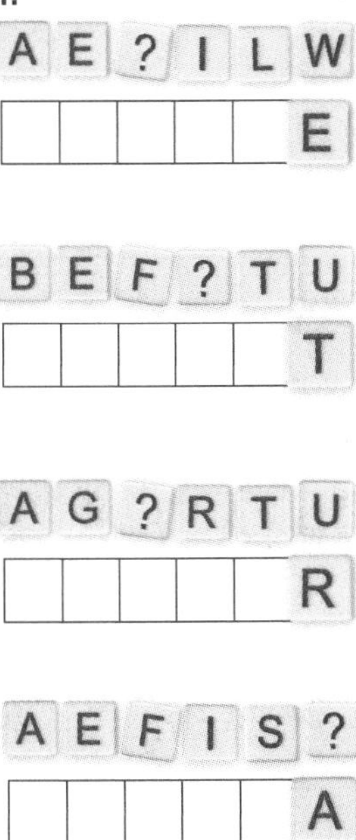

BANANA PEELS

There is one letter that when added to all of the five-letter words below can be used to form new six-letter words. Find the letter that works for all four words, add it to each word, and then rearrange each set of letters to form a new word. For example, B can be added to LOSS, ONLY, AUTO, and IRON to form SLOBS, NOBLY, ABOUT, and ROBIN.

COMMON LETTER

For each of the words below, replace one letter with the tile after the plus sign. Then rearrange the letters to spell something one wears.

B R I S K + T

☐☐☐☐☐

M O O I N G + K

☐☐☐☐☐☐

C R A S H + F

☐☐☐☐☐

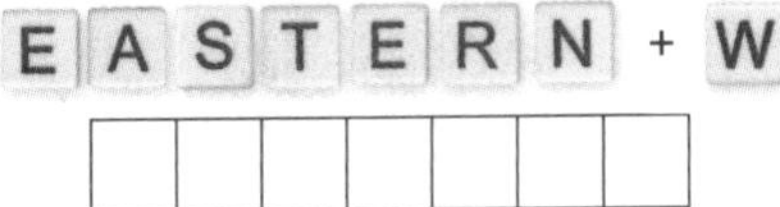

☐☐☐☐☐☐☐

Rearrange the tiles below to spell a six-letter word that fits in the first row. Then drop one letter and rearrange the remaining tiles to spell a five-letter word in the next row. Continue dropping one letter until you complete all five words. To get you started, one tile has been placed in each row.

A B E L M M

					M

		M		

	E		

		M

	E

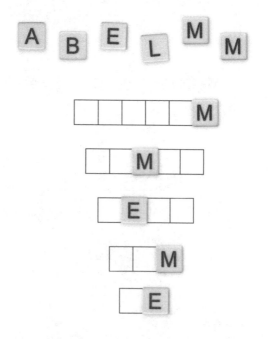

Using each three-letter word just once, combine a word in the left column with a word in the right column. Then rearrange each six-letter scramble to form a word that begins with an I, N, or A and write it into the appropriate space below.

AIM	PAL
LAP	ADO
BUN	MAN

I _ _ _ _ _

N _ _ _ _ _

A _ _ _ _ _

For the word group below, change one letter in the top word to one of the letters that appears in the bottom word, then rearrange the tiles to form a new common word. Do the same with each new word until you arrive at the bottom word.

For example, one path from BARK to PLUM is BARK, MARK, RAMP, RUMP, PLUM.

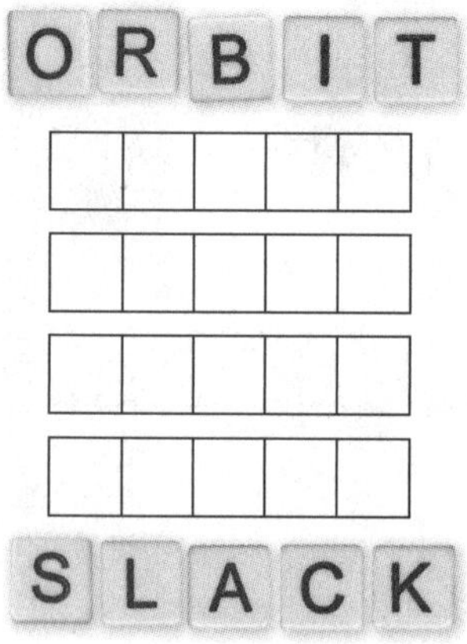

BUNCH OF BANANAS

For each word or phrase below, rearrange the letters to spell two parts of the human body. For example, SNORING FEE can be rearranged to spell NOSE, FINGER. The first letter of one word is placed to get you started.

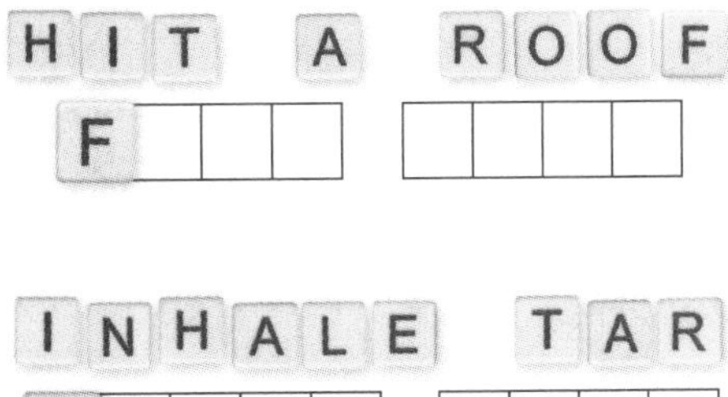

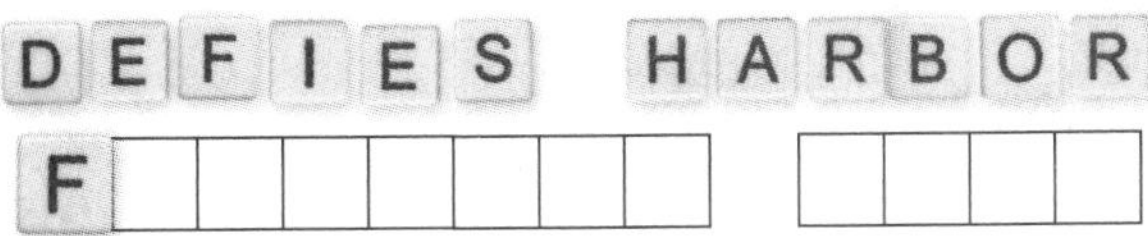

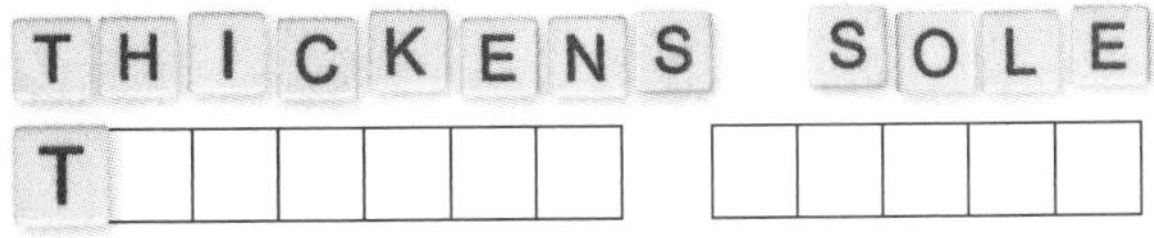

For each bunch below, rearrange the letters to form two intersecting words that fit into the corresponding grid.

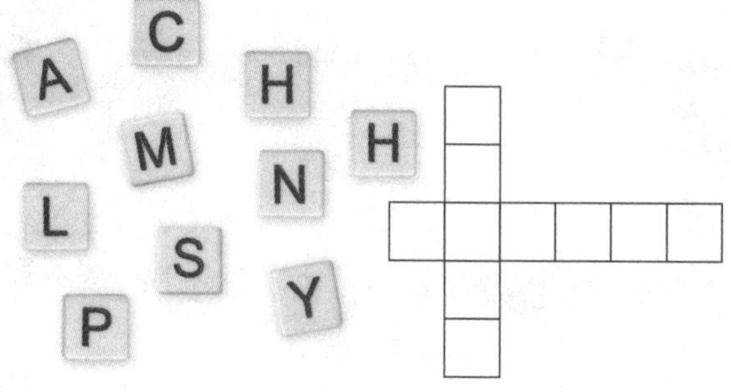

Each of the words below can be turned into another word on the list by changing one letter and then rearranging them all to form a new word. For example, REGIMENT can be turned into STEERING by changing the M to an S, so they would be a pair. How quickly can you find all the pairs?

1. GASLIT
2. PLURAL
3. AUTEUR
4. SATORI
5. FUTURE
6. ALLURE
7. SPITAL
8. TROIKA

Pairs

___ ___

___ ___

___ ___

___ ___

BANANA CRUNCH

LEVEL

Each set of 11 tiles contains one common five-letter word and one common six-letter word. The letters of the five-letter word are adjacent, but not in order. Find them and rearrange them to spell a word. Cross out those letters and rearrange the six remaining letters to spell the second word.

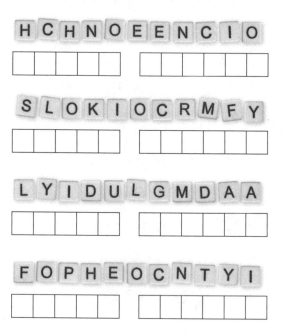

H C H N O E E N C I O

S L O K I O C R M F Y

L Y I D U L G M D A A

F O P H E O C N T Y I

Rearrange the letters of each word below and place them in the blanks so that, together with the two letters that have already been placed, they form a new word.

BANANA TREES

LEVEL

Use the 15 tiles in this bunch to create words that fit into the grids below. To get you started, a few tiles from the bunch have been placed in the grid. The BANANA BITES provide hints for one word to help you solve each grid. Reuse the 15 tiles in the bunch for each grid.

G O E S L R V

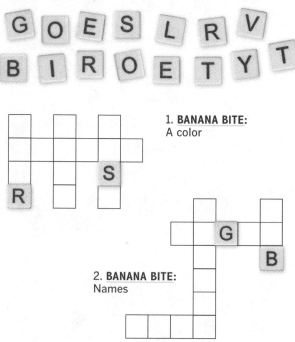

B I R O E T Y T

R S

1. **BANANA BITE:**
A color

G B

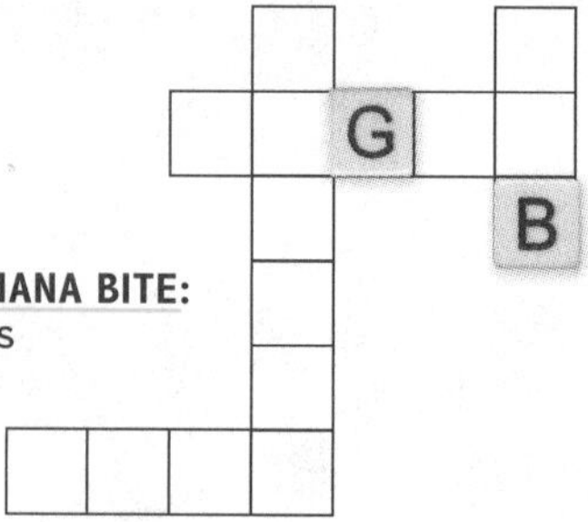

2. **BANANA BITE:**
Names

LEVEL

Each of the following six-letter sets can be rearranged to spell out a common word that either starts with M, N, or O or ends with G, H, or R. Find all the words as quickly as you can.

A A M N R T

E I N N T Y

B B E I L N

A D G I I N

C C O P U Y

A H M R T W

A G L R U V

C E E F N R

Add an R to each of the words below and then rearrange the letters in each word to form a new seven-letter word.

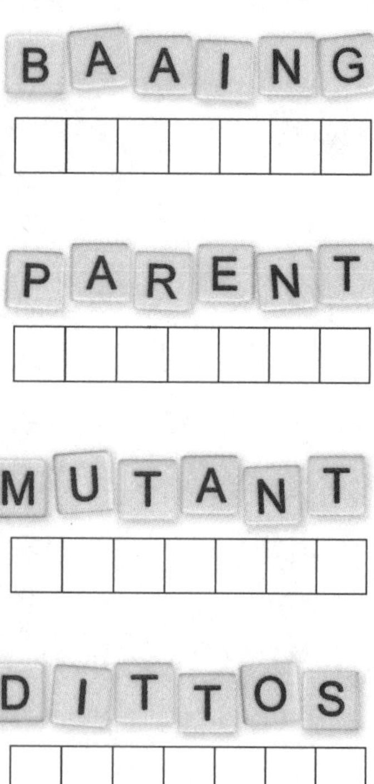

Each of the three-letter groups below may be extended on both the right and the left to form a seven-letter word. Drawing from the tiles directly above each group, fill in the blanks to find the words as quickly as you can.

LEVEL

In each puzzle, use four of the tiles from the bunch to fill in the blanks and make a seven-letter word that connects the grid.

A C B G H O T

SERVE
BRINE
BUG

BLUR
TREND
WEST

A C B D N O Y

BANANA CHIPS

Each set of letters is arranged alphabetically. The ? is in the correct alphabetical position. Figure out what letter the ? represents and rearrange the letters to spell a six-letter word that ends with the given letter. For example, in A?ENTV the ? could be an A, B, C, D, or E. Here it represents a D, which can be combined with the other letters to spell ADVENT.

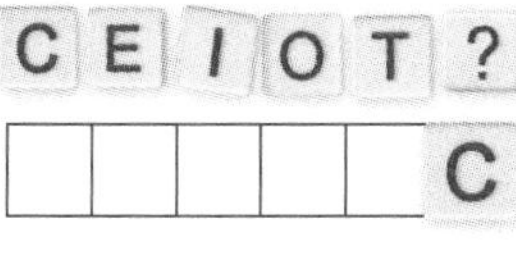

BANANA PEELS

There is one letter that when added to all of the five-letter words below can be used to form new six-letter words. Find the letter that works for all four words, add it to each word, and then rearrange each set of letters to form a new word. For example, B can be added to LOSS, ONLY, AUTO, and IRON to form SLOBS, NOBLY, ABOUT, and ROBIN.

COMMON LETTER

☐

E L D E R

☐☐☐☐☐☐

H A I L S

☐☐☐☐☐☐

T R E A D

☐☐☐☐☐☐

A C T O R

☐☐☐☐☐☐

For each of the words below, replace one letter with the tile after the plus sign. Then rearrange the letters to spell a type of food.

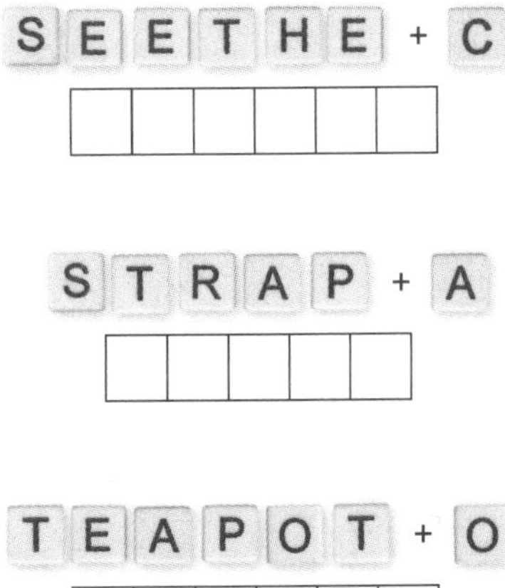

Rearrange the tiles below to spell a six-letter word that fits in the first row. Then drop one letter and rearrange the remaining tiles to spell a five-letter word in the next row. Continue dropping one letter until you complete all five words. To get you started, one tile has been placed in each row.

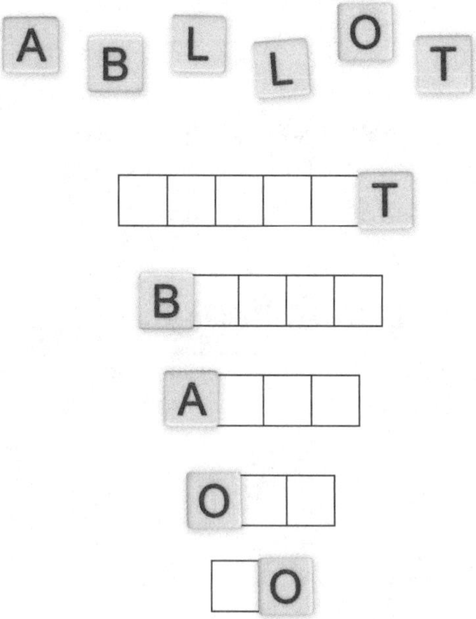

A B L L O T

_ _ _ _ _ T

B _ _ _ _

A _ _ _

O _ _

_ O

Using each three-letter word just once, combine a word in the left column with a word in the right column. Then rearrange each six-letter scramble to form a word that begins with a U, A, or T and write it into the appropriate space below.

A E T	P U B
V A T	P A T
C U E	I C E

U _ _ _ _ _

A _ _ _ _ _

T _ _ _ _ _

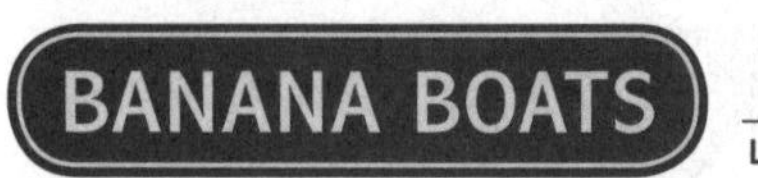

For the word group below, change one letter in the top word to one of the letters that appears in the bottom word, then rearrange the tiles to form a new common word. Do the same with each new word until you arrive at the bottom word.

For example, one path from BARK to PLUM is BARK, MARK, RAMP, RUMP, PLUM.

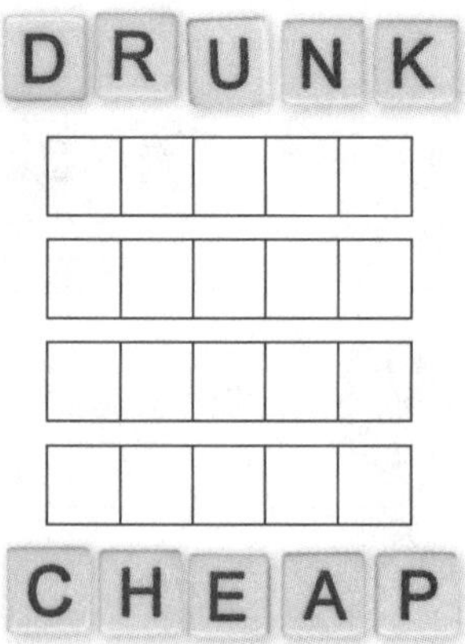

BUNCH OF BANANAS

For each word or phrase below, rearrange the letters to spell two things that are parts of a house. For example, CROP FLOATER can be rearranged to spell FLOOR, CARPET. The first letter of one word is placed to get you started.

KIN CALLERS

C _ _ _ _ _   _ _ _ _

RATS INVEST

V _ _ _   _ _ _ _ _ _

FOOTSY CREEK

S _ _ _ _ _   _ _ _ _ _

OPTIC CHART

P _ _ _ _   _ _ _ _ _

For each bunch below, rearrange the letters to form two intersecting words that fit into the corresponding grid.

A C D D E E O O W E

E A E E O O G W S Y

Each of the words below can be turned into another word on the list by changing one letter and then rearranging them all to form a new word. For example, REGIMENT can be turned into STEERING by changing the M to an S, so they would be a pair. How quickly can you find all the pairs?

1. BISECT
2. DEFIES
3. WEBLOG
4. SUBTLE
5. ICIEST
6. GOBLET
7. OBTUSE
8. BESIDE

Pairs

___ ___

___ ___

___ ___

___ ___

Each set of 11 tiles contains one common five-letter word and one common six-letter word. The letters of the five-letter word are adjacent, but not in order. Find them and rearrange them to spell a word. Cross out those letters and rearrange the six remaining letters to spell the second word.

N U T C I O G Y T M O

O P D E N F U L O U K

O M Y L E C C G U S E

E U M C N O B R M S U

Rearrange the letters of each word below and place them in the blanks so that, together with the two letters that have already been placed, they form a new word.

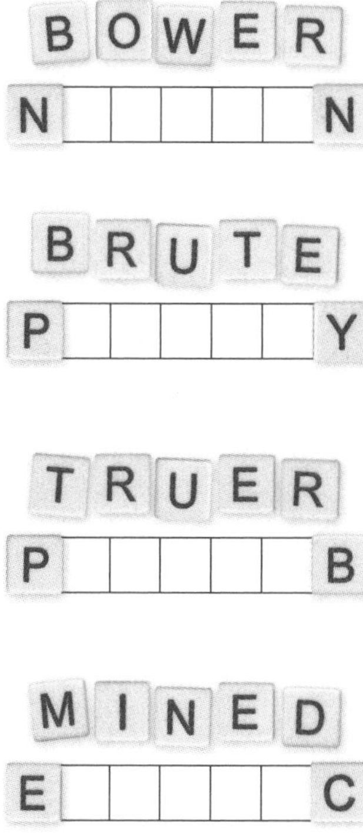

Use the 15 tiles in this bunch to create words that fit into the grids below. To get you started, a few tiles from the bunch have been placed in the grid. The BANANA BITES provide hints for one word to help you solve each grid. Reuse the 15 tiles in the bunch for each grid.

C R J A S W E
G A T Y E N Y T

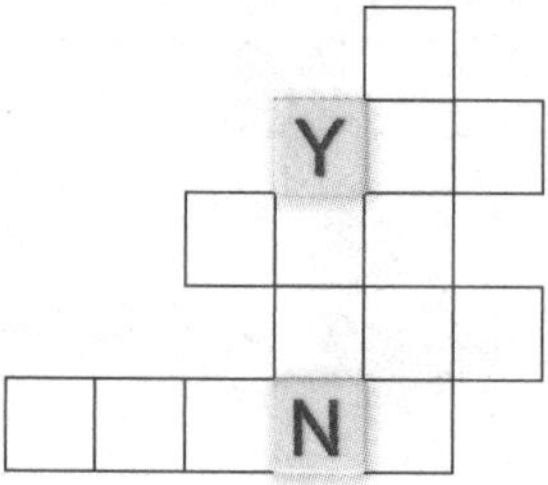

Y
N

1. **BANANA BITE:**
Animal enclosures

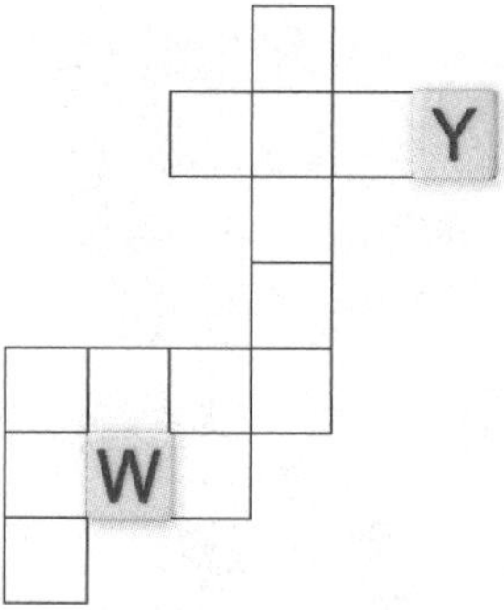

Y
W

2. **BANANA BITE:**
Birds

Each of the following six-letter sets can be rearranged to spell out a common word that either starts with A, G, or T and/or ends with D, E, or S. Find all the words as quickly as you can.

A C E E R S

D E E K S W

C E E I N T

A A C K T T

A C M P S U

A B G L L O

E L S S T U

C N O O T Y

Add a C to each of the words below and then rearrange the letters in each word to form a new seven-letter word.

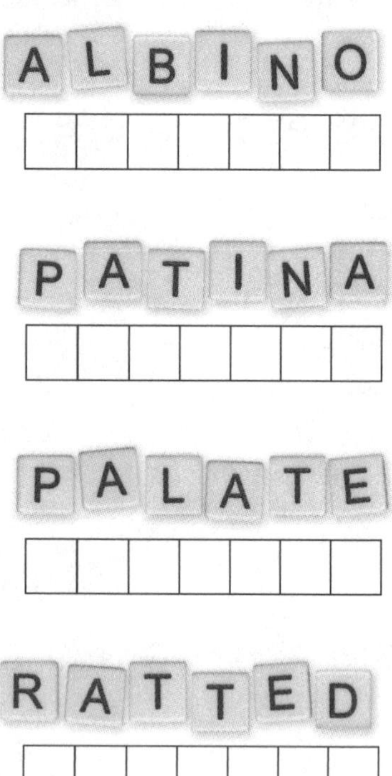

Each of the three-letter groups below may be extended on both the right and the left to form a seven-letter word. Drawing from the tiles directly above each group, fill in the blanks to find the words as quickly as you can.

BANANA LEAVES

LEVEL

In each puzzle, use four of the tiles from the bunch to fill in the blanks and make a seven-letter word that connects the grid.

E H E I N R T

UNDER

DARK

ACTOR

COLD

GLORY

OGRE

A E C L O R Y

Each set of letters is arranged alphabetically. The ? is in the correct alphabetical position. Figure out what letter the ? represents and rearrange the letters to spell a six-letter word that ends with the given letter. For example, in A?ENTV the ? could be an A, B, C, D, or E. Here it represents a D, which can be combined with the other letters to spell ADVENT.

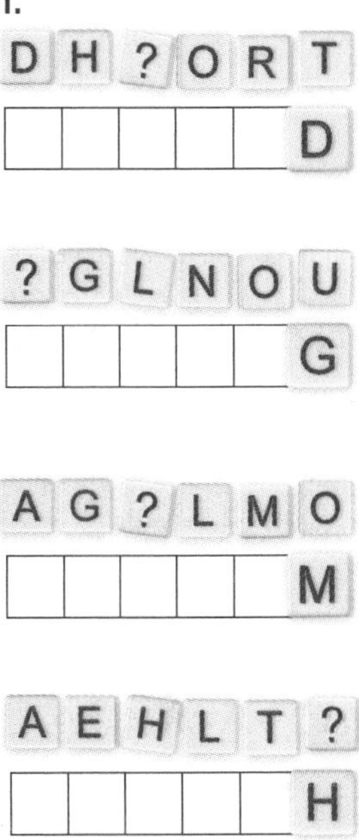

There is one letter that when added to all of the five-letter words below can be used to form new six-letter words. Find the letter that works for all four words, add it to each word, and then rearrange each set of letters to form a new word. For example, B can be added to LOSS, ONLY, AUTO, and IRON to form SLOBS, NOBLY, ABOUT, and ROBIN.

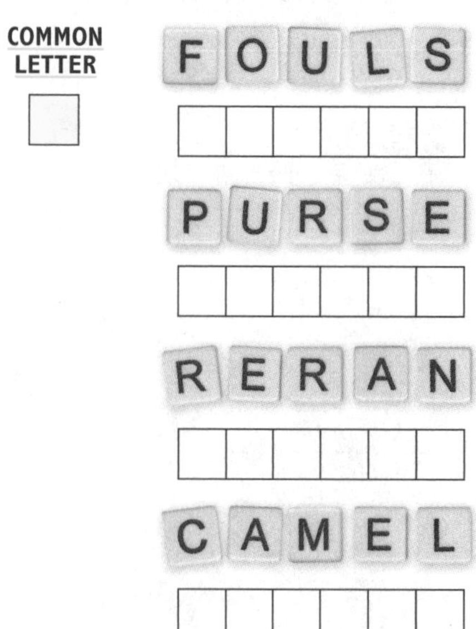

For each of the words below, replace one letter with the tile after the plus sign. Then rearrange the letters to spell an animal.

O R A T O R + P

B U T T E R + L

L E A G U E + B

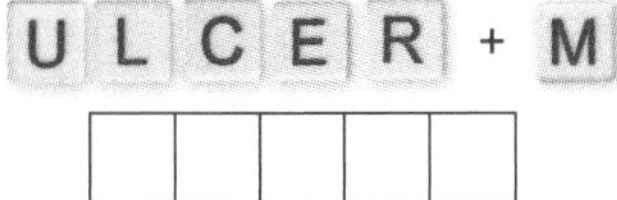

Rearrange the tiles below to spell a six-letter word that fits in the first row. Then drop one letter and rearrange the remaining tiles to spell a five-letter word in the next row. Continue dropping one letter until you complete all five words. To get you started, one tile has been placed in each row.

A C H K T W

_ _ _ A _ _

_ A _ _ _

C _ _ _

A _ _

A _

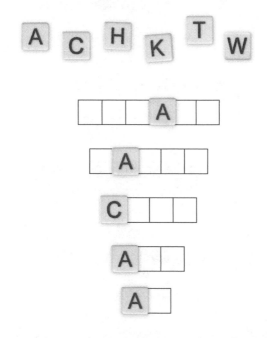

Using each three-letter word just once, combine a word in the left column with a word in the right column. Then rearrange each six-letter scramble to form a word that begins with an A, H, or T and write it into the appropriate space below.

COT	AIM
HEN	CUT
LAM	LAD

A _ _ _ _ _

H _ _ _ _ _

T _ _ _ _ _

For the word group below, change one letter in the top word to one of the letters that appears in the bottom word, then rearrange the tiles to form a new common word. Do the same with each new word until you arrive at the bottom word.

For example, one path from BARK to PLUM is BARK, MARK, RAMP, RUMP, PLUM.

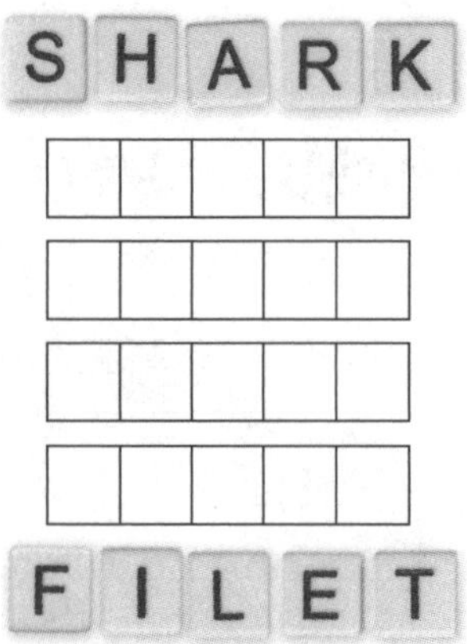

BUNCH OF BANANAS

LEVEL

For each word or phrase below, rearrange the letters to spell two nations. For example, PRYING SEAMAN can be rearranged to spell SPAIN, GERMANY. The first letter of one word is placed to get you started.

MAIN DAIRYMAN

M _ _ _ _ _ _   _ _ _ _ _

PARTY GUISES

E _ _ _ _   _ _ _ _ _ _

AIRPLANE NOMAD

P _ _ _ _ _   _ _ _ _ _ _ _

HAIL CHANGE

C _ _ _ _   _ _ _ _ _

For each bunch below, rearrange the letters to form two intersecting words that fit into the corresponding grid.

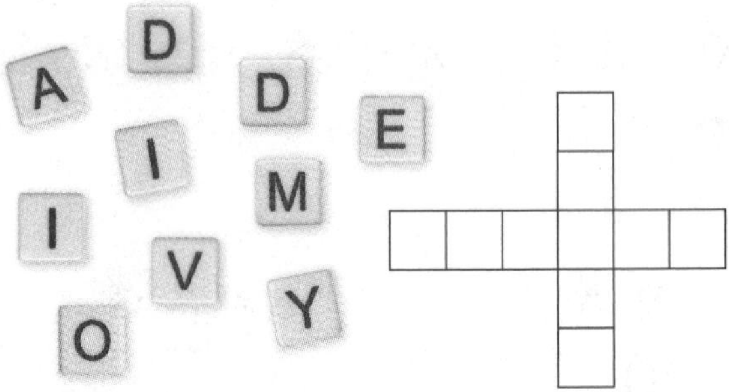

A E E L L N O V N Y

A D D I E I M V O Y

LEVEL

Each of the words below can be turned into another word on the list by changing one letter and then rearranging them all to form a new word. For example, REGIMENT can be turned into STEERING by changing the M to an S, so they would be a pair. How quickly can you find all the pairs?

1. C O E D I T
2. H E R E O F
3. R E F U S E
4. T R I O D E
5. C O O T I E
6. S E C U R E
7. P O E T I C
8. E C H O E R

Pairs

___ ___

___ ___

___ ___

___ ___

BANANA CRUNCH

LEVEL

Each set of 11 tiles contains one common five-letter word and one common six-letter word. The letters of the five-letter word are adjacent, but not in order. Find them and rearrange them to spell a word. Cross out those letters and rearrange the six remaining letters to spell the second word.

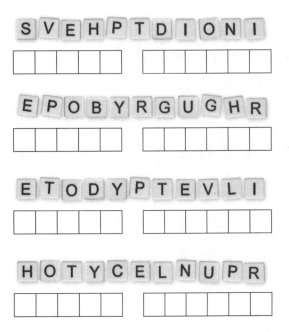

S V E H P T D I O N I

E P O B Y R G U G H R

E T O D Y P T E V L I

H O T Y C E L N U P R

Rearrange the letters of each word below and place them in the blanks so that, together with the two letters that have already been placed, they form a new word.

Use the 15 tiles in this bunch to create words that fit into the grids below. To get you started, a few tiles from the bunch have been placed in the grid. The BANANA BITES provide hints for one word to help you solve each grid. Reuse the 15 tiles in the bunch for each grid.

C F E A I F K
A D I J E L Z V

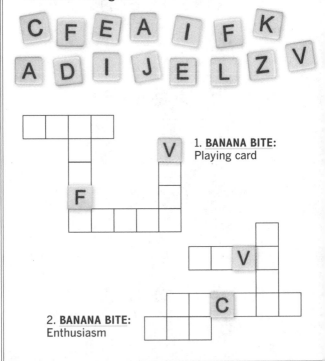

1. **BANANA BITE:**
Playing card

2. **BANANA BITE:**
Enthusiasm

LEVEL

Each of the following six-letter sets can be rearranged to spell out a common word that either starts with R, S, or W or ends with A, G, or R. Find all the words as quickly as you can.

A E O R T T

C D O O R T

A D E F O R

A E E R V W

B B D E G U

A E F S T Y

C E E L R V

A A N S T V

Add an M to each of the words below and then rearrange the letters in each word to form a new seven-letter word.

Each of the three-letter groups below may be extended on both the right and the left to form a seven-letter word. Drawing from the tiles directly above each group, fill in the blanks to find the words as quickly as you can.

In each puzzle, use four of the tiles from the bunch to fill in the blanks and make a seven-letter word that connects the grid.

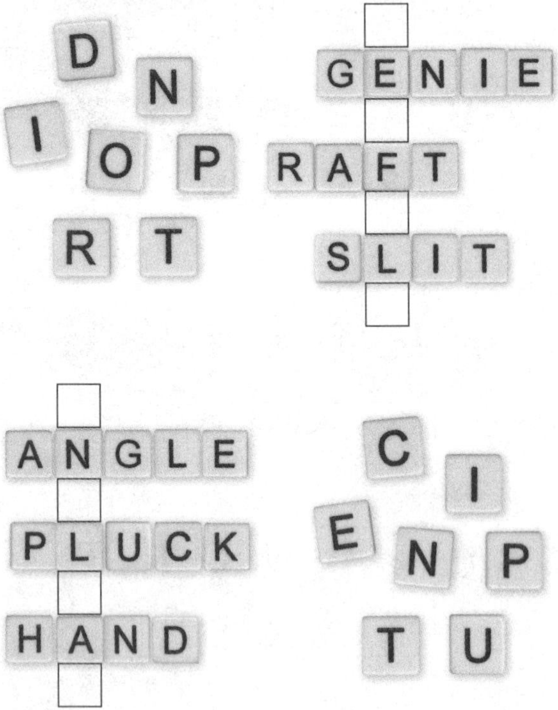

D N I O P R T

GENIE
RAFT
SLIT

ANGLE
PLUCK
HAND

C I E N P T U

Each set of letters is arranged alphabetically. The ? is in the correct alphabetical position. Figure out what letter the ? represents and rearrange the letters to spell a six-letter word that ends with the given letter. For example, in A?ENTV the ? could be an A, B, C, D, or E. Here it represents a D, which can be combined with the other letters to spell ADVENT.

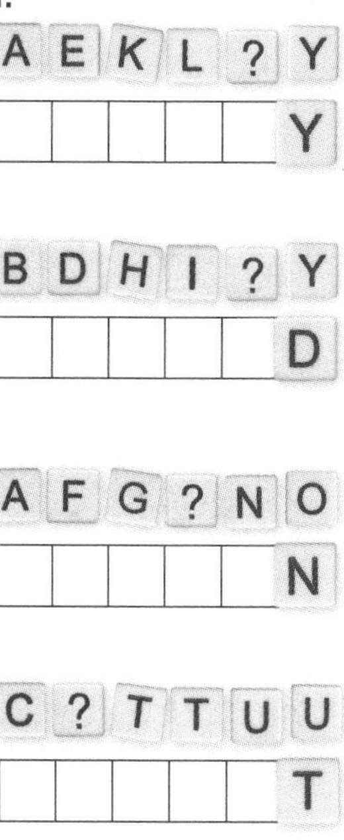

There is one letter that when added to all of the five-letter words below can be used to form new six-letter words. Find the letter that works for all four words, add it to each word, and then rearrange each set of letters to form a new word. For example, B can be added to LOSS, ONLY, AUTO, and IRON to form SLOBS, NOBLY, ABOUT, and ROBIN.

COMMON LETTER

☐

H O U R S

☐☐☐☐☐☐

L I G H T

☐☐☐☐☐☐

T E M P O

☐☐☐☐☐☐

F E I N T

☐☐☐☐☐☐

For each of the words below, replace one letter with the tile after the plus sign. Then rearrange the letters to spell a vacation destination.

A L I V E + L

C A B L E + H

R O U T E S + R

I N S U R E + C

Rearrange the tiles below to spell a six-letter word that fits in the first row. Then drop one letter and rearrange the remaining tiles to spell a five-letter word in the next row. Continue dropping one letter until you complete all five words. To get you started, one tile has been placed in each row.

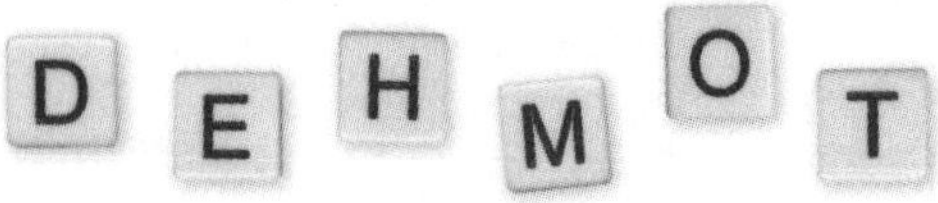

D E H M O T

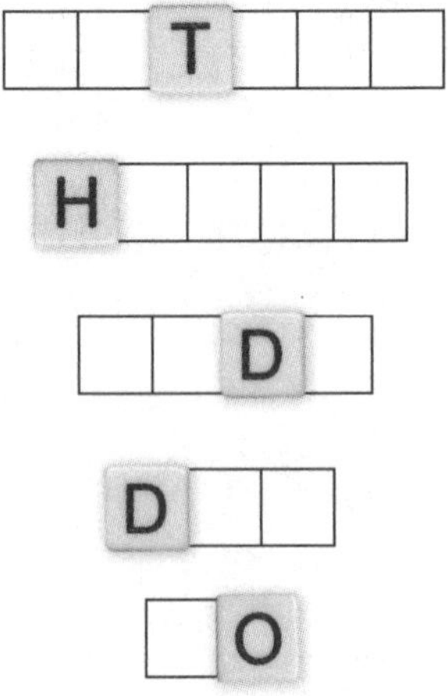

		T			

H				

		D	

D		

	O

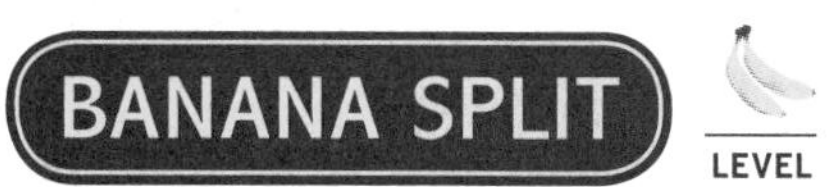

Using each three-letter word just once, combine a word in the left column with a word in the right column. Then rearrange each six-letter scramble to form a word that begins with an A, M, or T and write it into the appropriate space below.

AFT	TAD
DIM	RID
RUN	RAY

A _ _ _ _ _

M _ _ _ _ _

T _ _ _ _ _

For the word group below, change one letter in the top word to one of the letters that appears in the bottom word, then rearrange the tiles to form a new common word. Do the same with each new word until you arrive at the bottom word.

For example, one path from BARK to PLUM is BARK, MARK, RAMP, RUMP, PLUM.

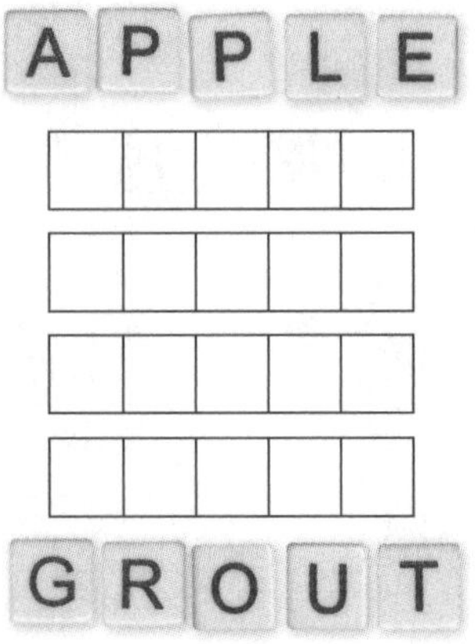

BUNCH OF BANANAS

LEVEL

For each word or phrase below, rearrange the letters to spell two words that are antonyms of each other. For example, RAKE LEAF can be rearranged to spell REAL, FAKE. The first letter of one word is placed to get you started.

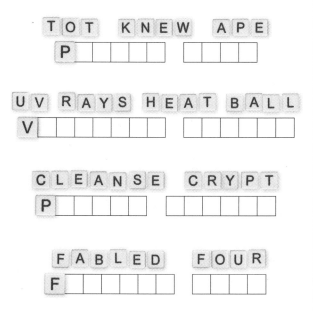

TOT KNEW APE

P _ _ _ _ _   _ _ _ _

UV RAYS HEAT BALL

V _ _ _ _ _ _ _   _ _ _ _ _ _

CLEANSE CRYPT

P _ _ _ _ _   _ _ _ _ _ _

FABLED FOUR

F _ _ _ _ _ _   _ _ _ _

For each bunch below, rearrange the letters to form two intersecting words that fit into the corresponding grid.

A A H I J M N R N S

H G A G S T L U U U

Each of the words below can be turned into another word on the list by changing one letter and then rearranging them all to form a new word. For example, REGIMENT can be turned into STEERING by changing the M to an S, so they would be a pair. How quickly can you find all the pairs?

1. L E N G T H
2. G R U N G E
3. N O O G I E
4. A L I G H T
5. G E N T L E
6. W I T H A L
7. U R G E N T
8. T O E I N G

Pairs

___ ___
___ ___
___ ___
___ ___

BANANA CRUNCH

LEVEL

Each set of 11 tiles contains one common five-letter word and one common six-letter word. The letters of the five-letter word are adjacent, but not in order. Find them and rearrange them to spell a word. Cross out those letters and rearrange the six remaining letters to spell the second word.

G O B I M L G T U N E

L I D N I C C Y R A A

O D E G H E M U M N S

O I R I Y L O D N U J

Rearrange the letters of each word below and place them in the blanks so that, together with the two letters that have already been placed, they form a new word.

LEVEL

Use the 15 tiles in this bunch to create words that fit into the grids below. To get you started, a few tiles from the bunch have been placed in the grid. The BANANA BITES provide hints for one word to help you solve each grid. Reuse the 15 tiles in the bunch for each grid.

A N E R D O E
L B O A U E N Z

1. **BANANA BITE:** Twice the amount

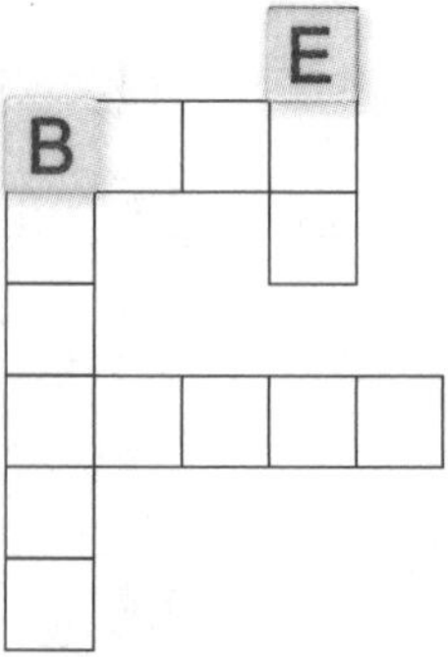

2. **BANANA BITE:** Twelve

BANANA SHAKES

LEVEL

Each of the following six-letter sets can be rearranged to spell out a common word that either starts with B, S, or U and/or ends with C, D, or H. Find all the words as quickly as you can.

C H L O S U

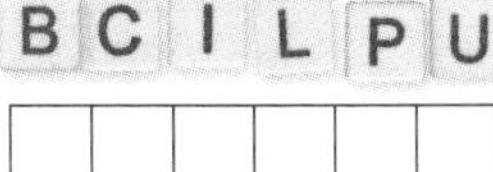

A G R S U Y

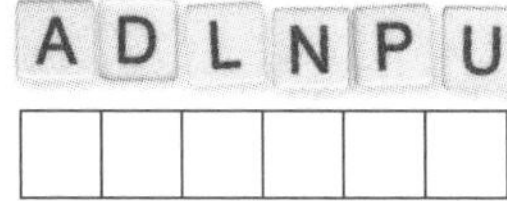

Add an N to each of the words below and then rearrange the letters in each word to form a new seven-letter word.

LEVEL

Each of the three-letter groups below may be extended on both the right and the left to form a seven-letter word. Drawing from the tiles directly above each group, fill in the blanks to find the words as quickly as you can.

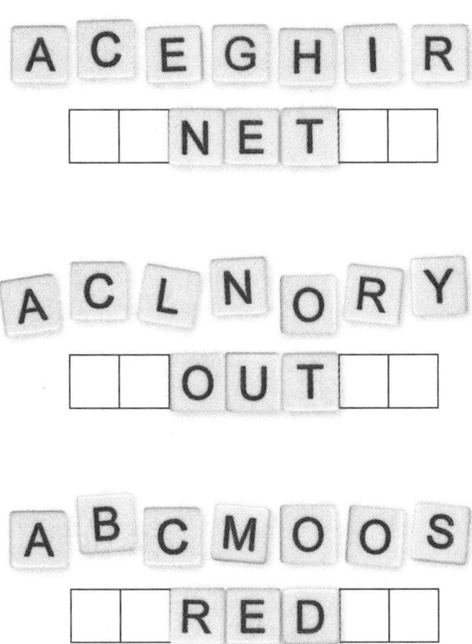

LEVEL

In each puzzle, use four of the tiles from the bunch to fill in the blanks and make a seven-letter word that connects the grid.

C I H N O P S

RUG
CATER
DONE

BURY
MADE
YOUNG

B G D M O P R

Each set of letters is arranged alphabetically. The ? is in the correct alphabetical position. Figure out what letter the ? represents and rearrange the letters to spell a six-letter word that ends with the given letter. For example, in A?ENTV the ? could be an A, B, C, D, or E. Here it represents a D, which can be combined with the other letters to spell ADVENT.

There is one letter that when added to all of the five-letter words below can be used to form new six-letter words. Find the letter that works for all four words, add it to each word, and then rearrange each set of letters to form a new word. For example, B can be added to LOSS, ONLY, AUTO and IRON to form SLOBS, NOBLY, ABOUT and ROBIN.

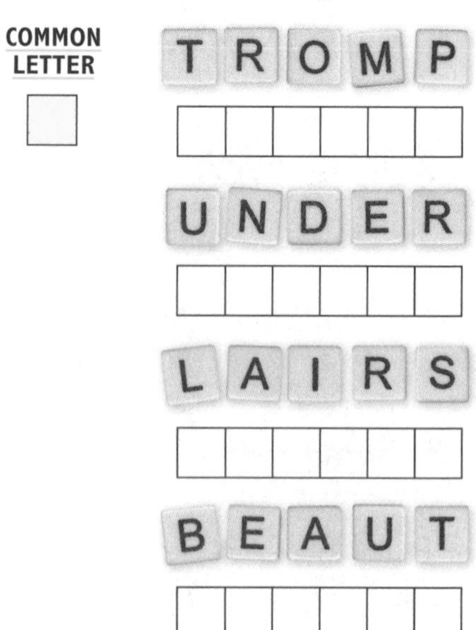

TOTALLY BANANAS

For each of the words below, replace one letter with the tile after the plus sign. Then rearrange the letters to spell a part of the body.

R A T I N G + E

P L A N E T + A

L A D E N + K

R E L I E D + Y

LEVEL

Rearrange the tiles below to spell a six-letter word that fits in the first row. Then drop one letter and rearrange the remaining tiles to spell a five-letter word in the next row. Continue dropping one letter until you complete all five words. To get you started, one tile has been placed in each row.

E O I M R O

_ _ _ M _ _

_ _ M _ _

R _ _ _

_ _ O

O _

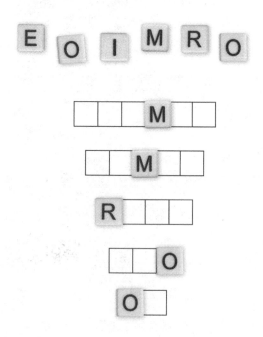

Using each three-letter word just once, combine a word in the left column with a word in the right column. Then rearrange each six-letter scramble to form a word that begins with an F or M and write it into the appropriate space below.

MAY RAG

OOH LAM

FLU POI

F _ _ _ _ _

M _ _ _ _ _

M _ _ _ _ _

For the word group below, change one letter in the top word to one of the letters that appears in the bottom word, then rearrange the tiles to form a new common word. Do the same with each new word until you arrive at the bottom word.

For example, one path from BARK to PLUM is BARK, MARK, RAMP, RUMP, PLUM.

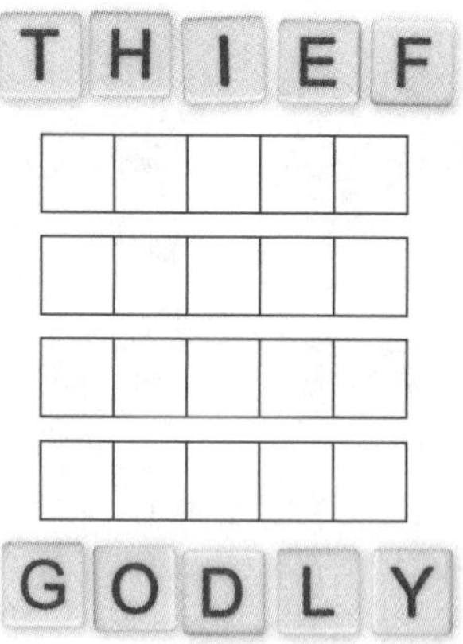

BUNCH OF BANANAS

LEVEL

For each word or phrase below, rearrange the letters to spell two words that are synonyms for each other. For example, SHOE CULTS can be rearranged to spell CLOSE, SHUT. The first letter of one word is placed to get you started.

TIGERS WANDER

W _ _ _ _   _ _ _ _ _ _ _

LOGGERS LOVE YOU

G _ _ _ _ _ _ _   _ _ _ _ _ _

TEEING SCARED

D _ _ _ _ _   _ _ _ _ _ _

LIMP SPANIEL

P _ _ _ _   _ _ _ _ _ _

For each bunch below, rearrange the letters to form two intersecting words that fit into the corresponding grid.

Each of the words below can be turned into another word on the list by changing one letter and then rearranging them all to form a new word. For example, REGIMENT can be turned into STEERING by changing the M to an S, so they would be a pair. How quickly can you find all the pairs?

1. C L O S E T
2. U N I S O N
3. M E D L E Y
4. A D R O I T
5. T R I P O D
6. E Y E L I D
7. C O U S I N
8. L O C U S T

Pairs

___ ___

___ ___

___ ___

___ ___

LEVEL

Each set of 11 tiles contains one common five-letter word and one common six-letter word. The letters of the five-letter word are adjacent, but not in order. Find them and rearrange them to spell a word. Cross out those letters and rearrange the six remaining letters to spell the second word.

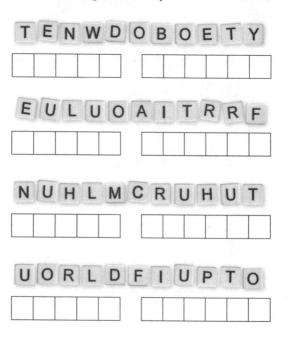

T E N W D O B O E T Y

E U L U O A I T R R F

N U H L M C R U H U T

U O R L D F I U P T O

Rearrange the letters of each word below and place them in the blanks so that, together with the two letters that have already been placed, they form a new word.

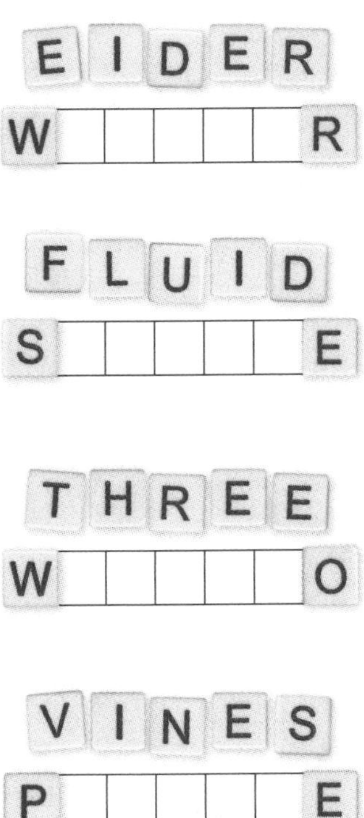

BANANA TREES

LEVEL

Use the 15 tiles in this bunch to create words that fit into the grids below. To get you started, a few tiles from the bunch have been placed in the grid. The BANANA BITES provide hints for one word to help you solve each grid. Reuse the 15 tiles in the bunch for each grid.

D O I E W N S
G N D Q X U E W

1. **BANANA BITE:**
A number

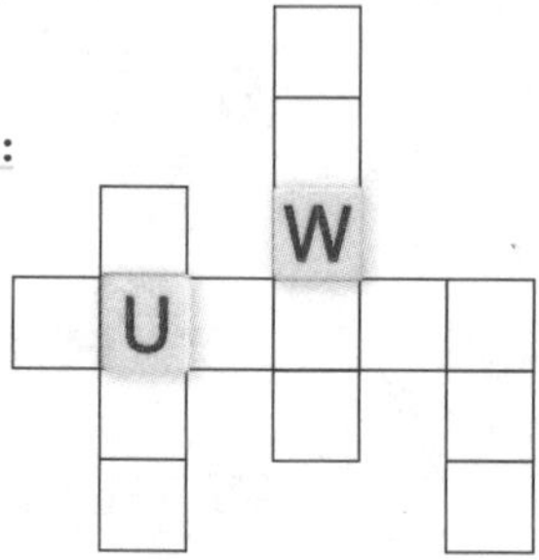

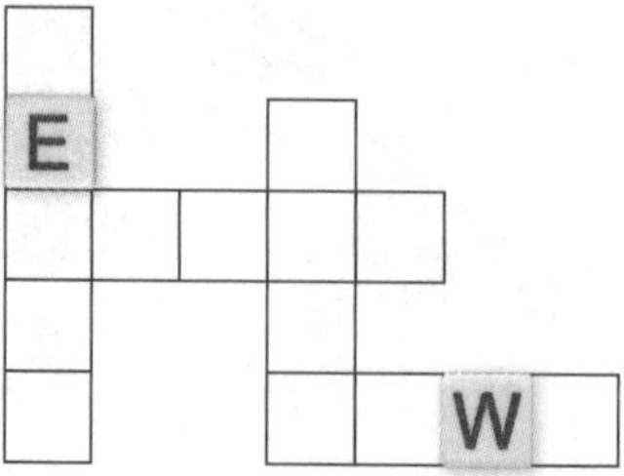

U W

E W

2. **BANANA BITE:**
Tentacled creature

LEVEL

Each of the following six-letter sets can be rearranged to spell out a common word that either starts with C, P, or T and/or ends with N, S, or T. Find all the words as quickly as you can.

A C E O R S

A N N S T U

A B E E N T

A E N N T T

E G I L P T

A C E K P T

A D I R S U

C D E I N R

Add an L to each of the words below and then rearrange the letters in each word to form a new seven-letter word.

Each of the three-letter groups below may be extended on both the right and the left to form a seven-letter word. Drawing from the tiles directly above each group, fill in the blanks to find the words as quickly as you can.

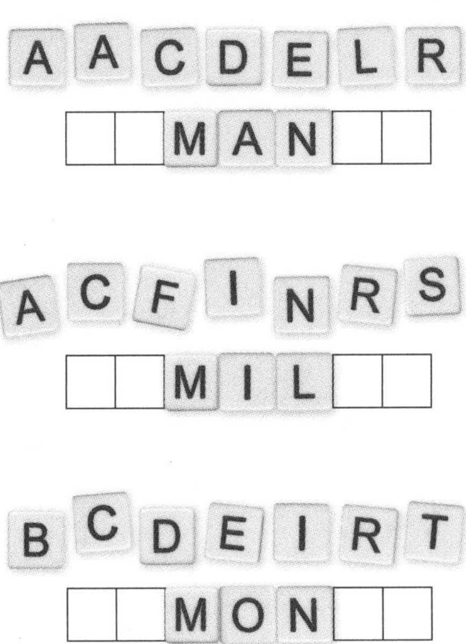

LEVEL

In each puzzle, use four of the tiles from the bunch to fill in the blanks and make a seven-letter word that connects the grid.

C M L N P R T

	O			
L	O	A	D	
	_			
N	E	C	K	
	_			
P	A	N	D	A
	_			

Top: _

	_			
W	O	U	L	D
	_			
V	I	N	E	
	_			
M	U	G		
	_			

C M D M N R T

Each set of letters is arranged alphabetically. The ? is in the correct alphabetical position. Figure out what letter the ? represents and rearrange the letters to spell a six-letter word that ends with the given letter. For example, in A?ENTV the ? could be an A, B, C, D, or E. Here it represents a D, which can be combined with the other letters to spell ADVENT.

There is <u>one letter</u> that when added to all of the five-letter words below can be used to form new six-letter words. Find the letter that works for all four words, add it to each word, and then rearrange each set of letters to form a new word. For example, B can be added to LOSS, ONLY, AUTO, and IRON to form SLOBS, NOBLY, ABOUT, and ROBIN.

COMMON LETTER

☐

R O U G E

☐☐☐☐☐☐

R E U S E

☐☐☐☐☐☐

S O A R S

☐☐☐☐☐☐

L O A N S

☐☐☐☐☐☐

TOTALLY BANANAS

LEVEL

For each of the words below, replace one letter with the tile after the plus sign. Then rearrange the letters to spell a type of container.

O U T L E T + B

R A T I O N + C

C O P T E R + K

D O S E + H

LEVEL

Rearrange the tiles below to spell a six-letter word that fits in the first row. Then drop one letter and rearrange the remaining tiles to spell a five-letter word in the next row. Continue dropping one letter until you complete all five words. To get you started, one tile has been placed in each row.

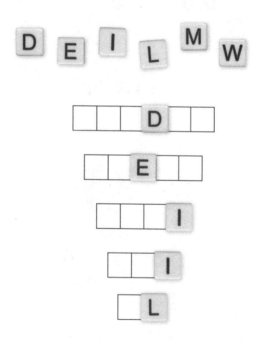

D E I L M W

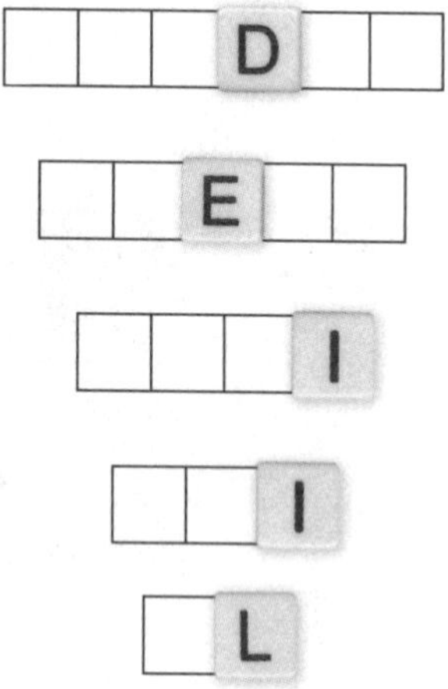

| | | | D | | |

| | | E | | |

| | | | I |

| | | I |

| | L |

Using each three-letter word just once, combine a word in the left column with a word in the right column. Then rearrange each six-letter scramble to form a word that begins with a T, H, or N and write it into the appropriate space below.

T A T	E R G
N U T	E L M
H A T	E A R

T _ _ _ _ _

H _ _ _ _ _

N _ _ _ _ _

For the word group below, change one letter in the top word to one of the letters that appears in the bottom word, then rearrange the tiles to form a new common word. Do the same with each new word until you arrive at the bottom word.

For example, one path from BARK to PLUM is BARK, MARK, RAMP, RUMP, PLUM.

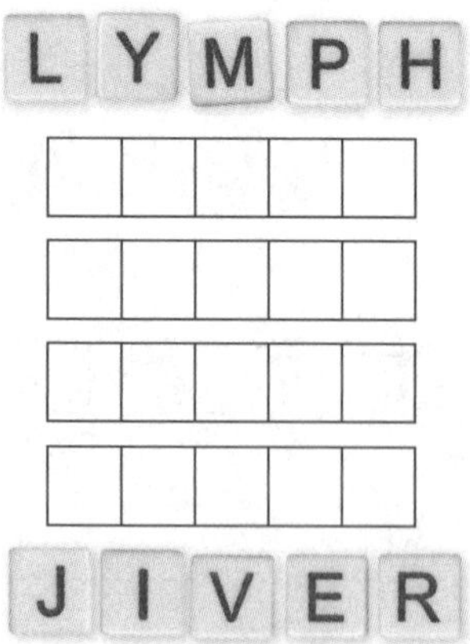

BUNCH OF BANANAS

LEVEL

For each word or phrase below, rearrange the letters to spell the last names of actors who had a romance together in a famous movie. For example, ABOUNDING LEGS can be rearranged to spell Michael DOUGLAS, Annette BENING (*The American President*).

BIG LEG HEAL

☐☐☐☐☐ ☐☐☐☐☐

TAR BOMBER GANG

☐☐☐☐☐☐ ☐☐☐☐☐☐☐

WARM ZOO EYES

☐☐☐☐☐☐ ☐☐☐☐☐

WEIRDO IN PLASTIC

☐☐☐☐☐☐☐☐ ☐☐☐☐☐☐☐

For each bunch below, rearrange the letters to form two intersecting words that fit into the corresponding grid.

A A F G H L P R N U U

A D G H O H L O O P R

Each of the words below can be turned into another word on the list by changing one letter and then rearranging them all to form a new word. For example, REGIMENT can be turned into STEERING by changing the M to an S, so they would be a pair. How quickly can you find all the pairs?

1. F A N A T I C
2. S T A M I N A
3. E A R T H E N
4. D I E T A R Y
5. A N I M A T E
6. A I R D A T E
7. C A P T A I N
8. B E N E A T H

Pairs

___ ___

___ ___

___ ___

___ ___

Each set of 12 tiles contains two common six-letter words. The letters of the first six-letter word are adjacent, but not in order. Find them and rearrange them to spell a word. Cross out those letters and rearrange the six remaining letters to spell the second word.

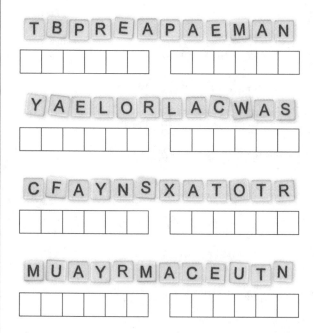

T B P R E A P A E M A N

Y A E L O R L A C W A S

C F A Y N S X A T O T R

M U A Y R M A C E U T N

Rearrange the letters of each word below and place them in the blanks so that, together with the two letters that have already been placed, they form a new word.

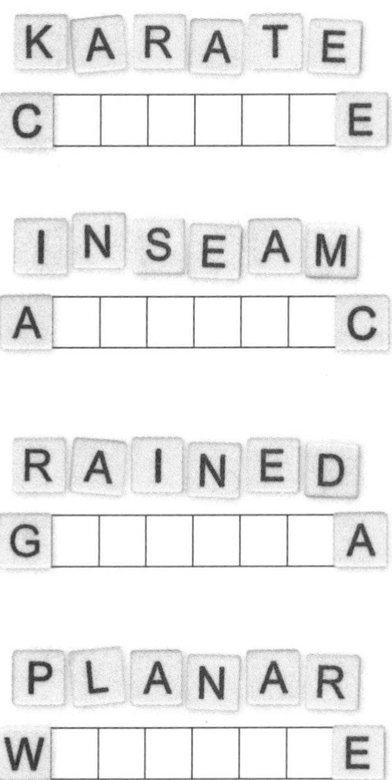

Use the 15 tiles in this bunch to create words that fit into the grids below. To get you started, a few tiles from the bunch have been placed in the grid. Reuse the 15 tiles in the bunch for each grid.

I A R E O A T

B N L A I T U H

B

T O

L

I

O U

I

Each of the following seven-letter sets can be rearranged to spell out a common word that either starts with B E or D E or ends with N T or O N. Find all the words as quickly as you can.

A B E G I N O

A F F N O R T

A B N O T U Y

D E G N N O U

A A G N O P R

A A D D E N P

A D E I I L R

B E H L L O P

Add an H to each of the words below and then rearrange the letters in each word to form a new seven-letter word.

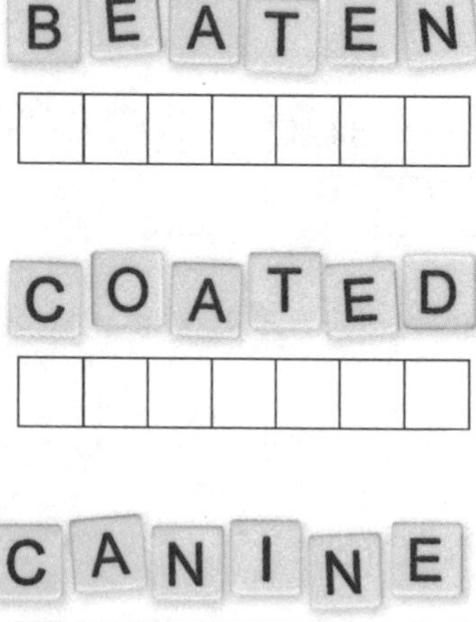

Each of the four-letter groups below may be extended on both the right and the left to form an eight-letter word. Drawing from the tiles directly above each group, fill in the blanks to find the words as quickly as you can.

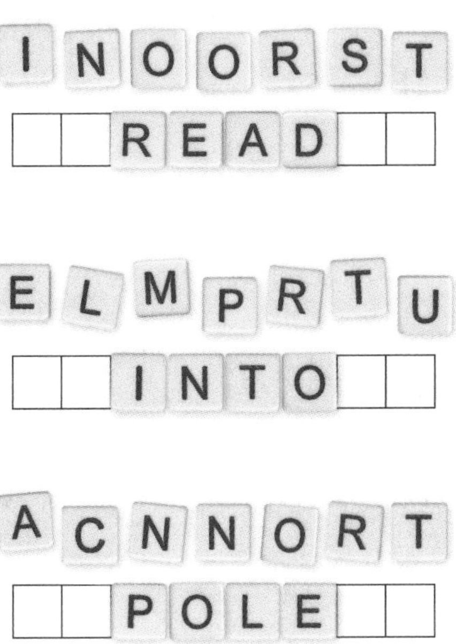

BANANA LEAVES

LEVEL

In each puzzle, use four of the tiles from the bunch to fill in the blanks and make an eight-letter word that connects the grid.

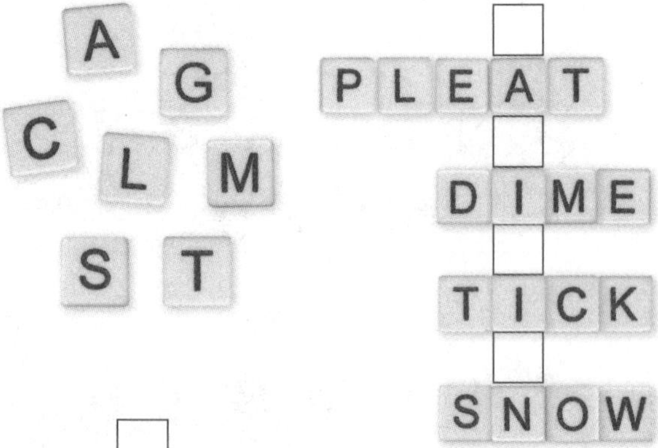

A G C L M S T

PLEAT
DIME
TICK
SNOW

PARTY
ACTOR
FANG
GROWL

A E B H I M O

Each set of letters is arranged alphabetically. The ? is in the correct alphabetical position. Figure out what letter the ? represents and rearrange the letters to spell a seven-letter word that begins with the given letter. For example, in AAIN?TV the ? could be an N, O, P, Q, R, S, or T. Here it represents an R, which can be combined with the other letters to spell VARIANT.

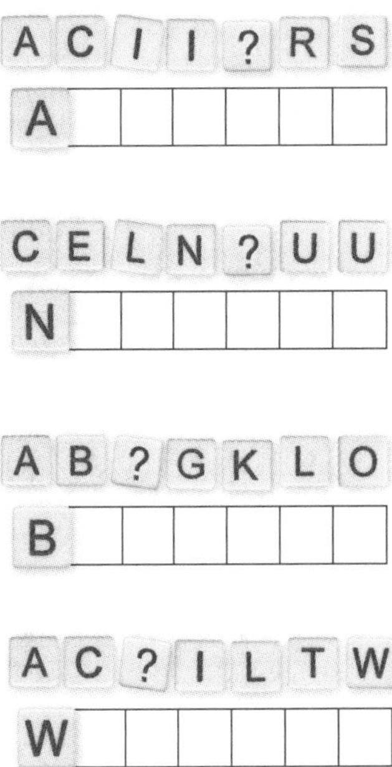

There is <u>one letter</u> that when added to all of the six-letter words below can be used to form new seven-letter words. Find the letter that works for all four words, add it to each word, and then rearrange each set of letters to form a new word. For example, B can be added to LOSS, ONLY, AUTO, and IRON to form SLOBS, NOBLY, ABOUT, and ROBIN.

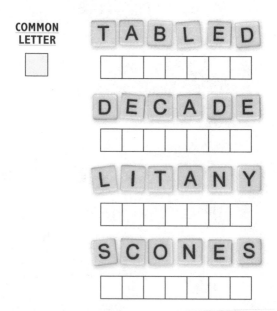

COMMON LETTER

T A B L E D

D E C A D E

L I T A N Y

S C O N E S

For each of the words below, replace one letter with the tile after the plus sign. Then rearrange the letters to spell a type of TV show or movie.

M A G E N T A + P

Z Y D E C O + M

C A T N I P + O

Rearrange the tiles below to spell a seven-letter word that fits in the first row. Then drop one letter and rearrange the remaining tiles to spell a six-letter word in the next row. Continue dropping one letter until you complete all six words. To get you started, one tile has been placed in each row.

A C C E L N O

			C			

					L

		N		

	C	

		N

A	

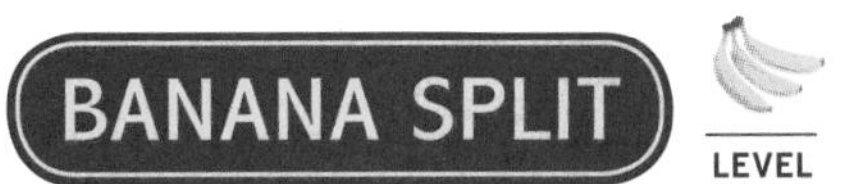

Using each four- and three-letter word just once, combine a word in the left column with a word in the right column. Then rearrange each seven-letter scramble to form a word that begins with an L, G, or B and write it into the appropriate space below.

DRAG	RAN
GOAL	GAL
HARD	BET

L _ _ _ _ _ _

G _ _ _ _ _ _

B _ _ _ _ _ _

For the word group below, change one letter in the top word to one of the letters that appears in the bottom word, then rearrange the tiles to form a new common word. Do the same with each new word until you arrive at the bottom word.

For example, one path from BARK to PLUM is BARK, MARK, RAMP, RUMP, PLUM.

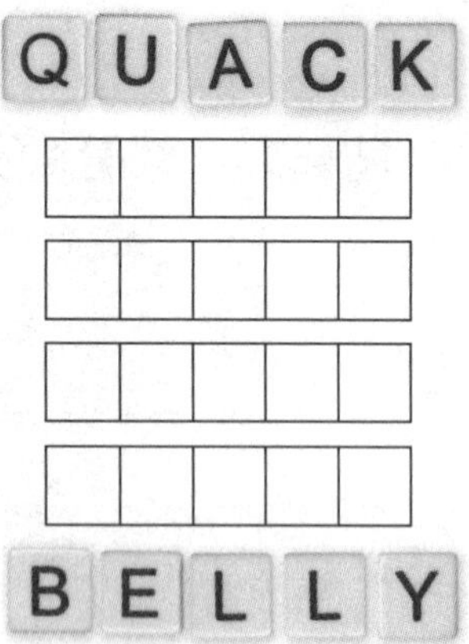

BUNCH OF BANANAS

For each word or phrase below, rearrange the letters to spell two musical instruments. For example, FEEL TRULY can be rearranged to spell FLUTE, LYRE.

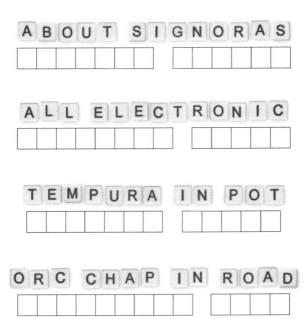

ABOUT SIGNORAS

ALL ELECTRONIC

TEMPURA IN POT

ORC CHAP IN ROAD

For each bunch below, rearrange the letters to form two intersecting words that fit into the corresponding grid.

A A C D O R T V R Y W

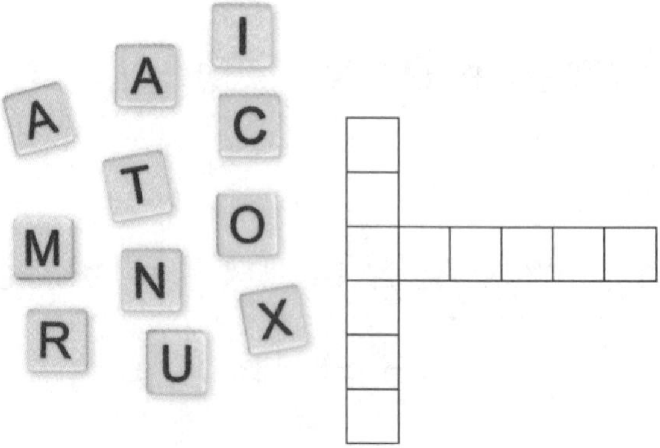

A I A C T O M N R U X

Each of the words below can be turned into another word on the list by changing one letter and then rearranging them all to form a new word. For example, REGIMENT can be turned into STEERING by changing the M to an S, so they would be a pair. How quickly can you find all the pairs?

1. ABOLISH
2. BONDAGE
3. EDUCATE
4. CHABLIS
5. CLIMATE
6. SAUTEED
7. DECAGON
8. ETHICAL

Pairs

___ ___

___ ___

___ ___

___ ___

Each set of 12 tiles contains two common six-letter words. The letters of the first six-letter word are adjacent, but not in order. Find them and rearrange them to spell a word. Cross out those letters and rearrange the six remaining letters to spell the second word.

C A U R P A W N L A F I

C T U G N D A A E A S C

R R O A B E O G Z T A O

W M U M L A G O B P A R

Rearrange the letters of each word below and place them in the blanks so that, together with the two letters that have already been placed, they form a new word.

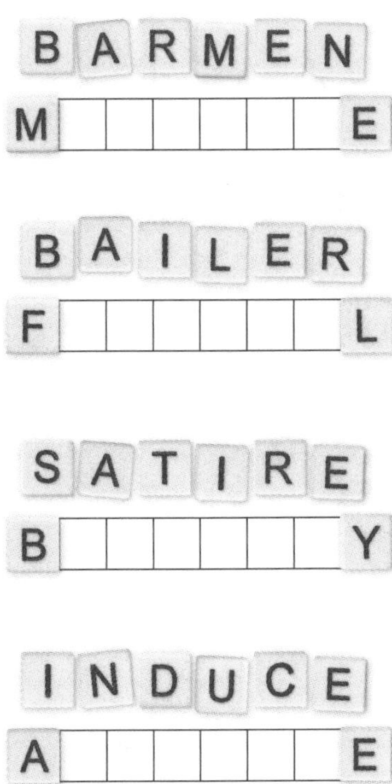

Use the 15 tiles in this bunch to create words that fit into the grids below. To get you started, a few tiles from the bunch have been placed in the grid. Reuse the 15 tiles in the bunch for each grid.

B G A E L R O

A H D M O V T Z

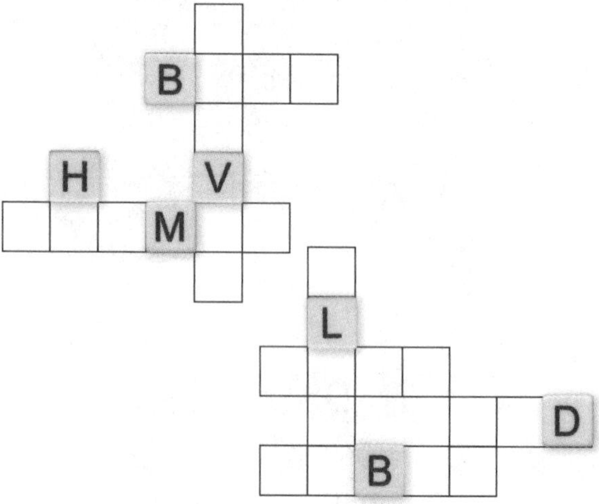

B

H V

M

L

D

B

LEVEL

Each of the following seven-letter sets can be rearranged to spell out a common word that either starts with E N or P R or ends with I C or T E. Find all the words as quickly as you can.

A C E E F P R

C E E L N O S

A A E G I T T

C C D E I M O

B E E L N N O

D E E I R T U

A C C E I S T

A C I P R V Y

LEVEL

Add a W to each of the words below and then rearrange the letters in each word to form a new seven-letter word.

Each of the four-letter groups below may be extended on both the right and the left to form an eight-letter word. Drawing from the tiles directly above each group, fill in the blanks to find the words as quickly as you can.

In each puzzle, use four of the tiles from the bunch to fill in the blanks and make an eight-letter word that connects the grid.

Tiles: D M L N P R Z

		_		
T	H	A	N	K
		_		
	Z	A	P	
		_		
W	H	Y		
		_		
	L	E	A	F

	_			
S	H	O	T	
	_			
O	P	T	I	C
	_			
B	E	N	D	
	_			
O	D	D	L	Y

Tiles: C H E L N R S

Each set of letters is arranged alphabetically. The ? is in the correct alphabetical position. Figure out what letter the ? represents and rearrange the letters to spell a seven-letter word that begins with the given letter. For example, in AAIN?TV the ? could be an N, O, P, Q, R, S, or T. Here it represents an R, which can be combined with the other letters to spell VARIANT.

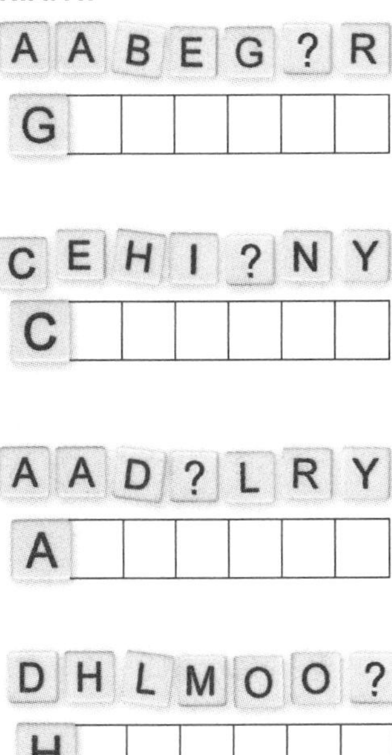

There is <u>one letter</u> that when added to all of the six-letter words below can be used to form new seven-letter words. Find the letter that works for all four words, add it to each word, and then rearrange each set of letters to form a new word. For example, B can be added to LOSS, ONLY, AUTO, and IRON to form SLOBS, NOBLY, ABOUT, and ROBIN.

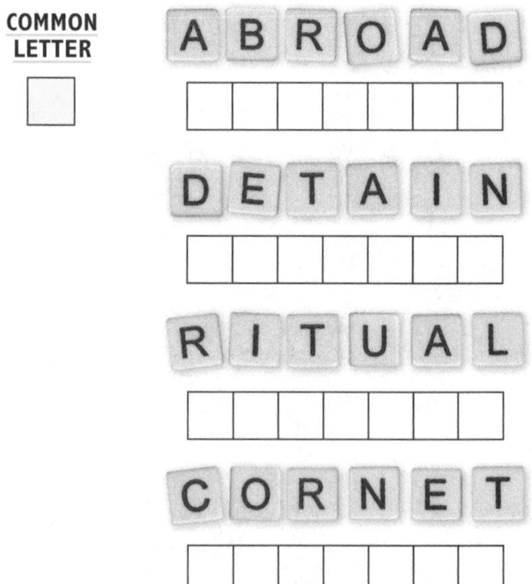

For each of the words below, replace one letter with the tile after the plus sign. Then rearrange the letters to spell a type of fish.

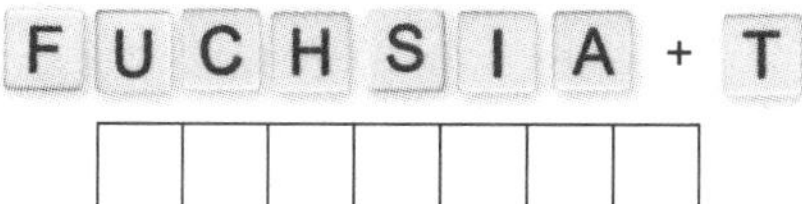

T A B O U L I + H

Rearrange the tiles below to spell a seven-letter word that fits in the first row. Then drop one letter and rearrange the remaining tiles to spell a six-letter word in the next row. Continue dropping one letter until you complete all six words. To get you started, one tile has been placed in each row.

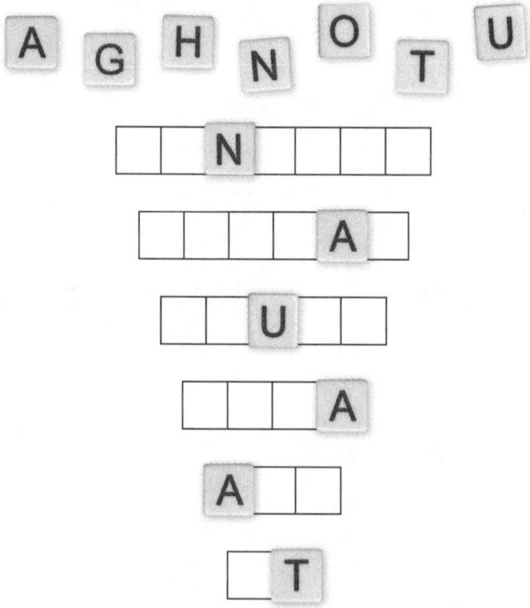

A G H N O T U

		N				

				A	

		U		

			A

A		

	T

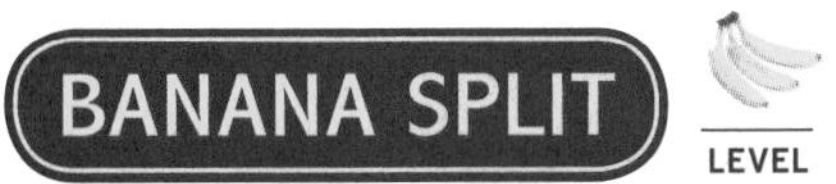

Using each four- and three-letter word just once, combine a word in the left column with a word in the right column. Then rearrange each seven-letter scramble to form a word that begins with an A, S, or E and write it into the appropriate space below.

ABLE	LYE
BANS	HUT
HAVE	ICE

A _ _ _ _ _ _

S _ _ _ _ _ _

E _ _ _ _ _ _

For the word group below, change one letter in the top word to one of the letters that appears in the bottom word, then rearrange the tiles to form a new common word. Do the same with each new word until you arrive at the bottom word.

For example, one path from BARK to PLUM is BARK, MARK, RAMP, RUMP, PLUM.

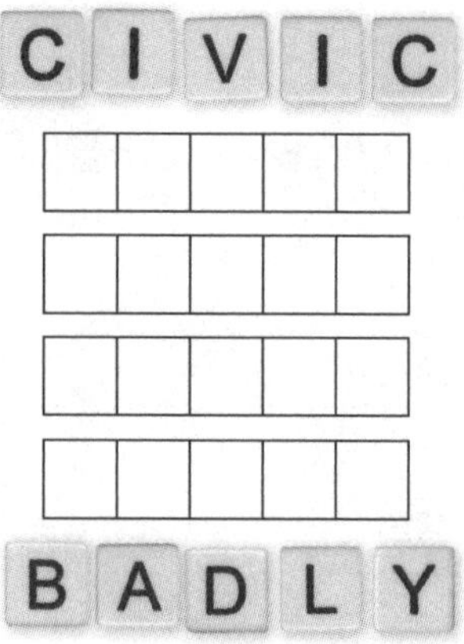

BUNCH OF BANANAS

For each word or phrase below, rearrange the letters to spell two words that appear in the titles of different Beatles songs. For example, TRY BRIAR WATERS can be rearranged to spell "STRAWBERRY Fields," "Lovely RITA."

MERRY TEENY SHOW

NAKED MINT TACO

SNOW A REAL LURE

DEFRAGS DINNER

For each bunch below, rearrange the letters to form two intersecting words that fit into the corresponding grid.

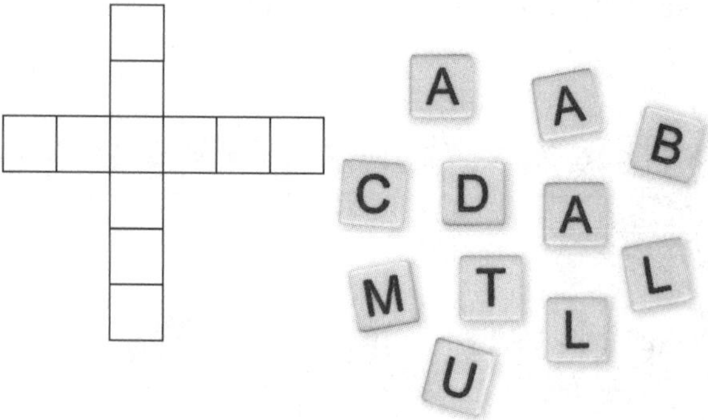

A A B C D A M T L L U

A A A C D C D F E I N

Each of the words below can be turned into another word on the list by changing one letter and then rearranging them all to form a new word. For example, REGIMENT can be turned into STEERING by changing the M to an S, so they would be a pair. How quickly can you find all the pairs?

1. L I V E N E D
2. O U T E A R N
3. S U N D I A L
4. R E T R E A D
5. E V I D E N T
6. N E U T R A L
7. M A U D L I N
8. A E R A T E D

Pairs

___ ___

___ ___

___ ___

___ ___

Each set of 12 tiles contains two common six-letter words. The letters of the first six-letter word are adjacent, but not in order. Find them and rearrange them to spell a word. Cross out those letters and rearrange the six remaining letters to spell the second word.

M L L F A B E C D A A P

O L A N B S A P R U C A

U E A E K H A N I P N T

E Y A H M P S I K D P A

Rearrange the letters of each word below and place them in the blanks so that, together with the two letters that have already been placed, they form a new word.

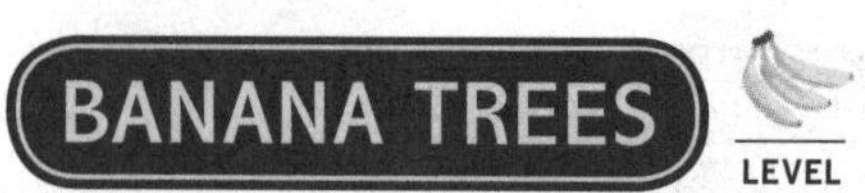

Use the 15 tiles in this bunch to create words that fit into the grids below. To get you started, a few tiles from the bunch have been placed in the grid. Reuse the 15 tiles in the bunch for each grid.

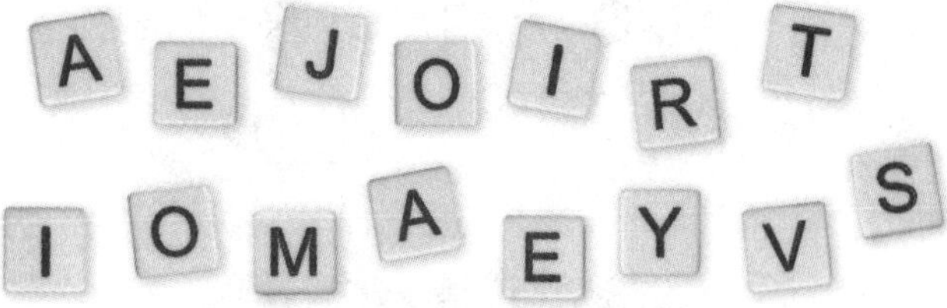

A E J O I R T

I O M A E Y V S

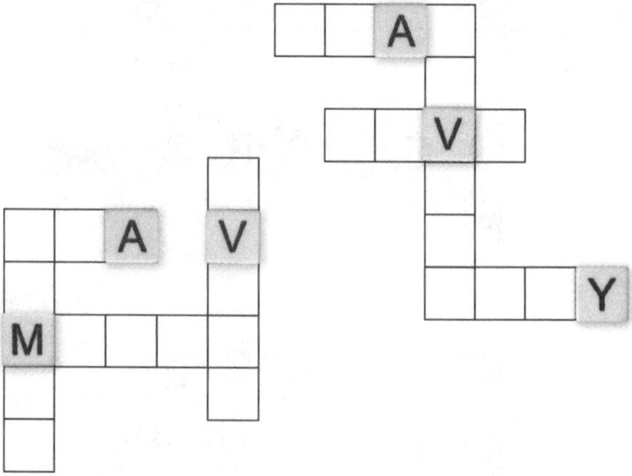

LEVEL

Each of the following seven-letter sets can be rearranged to spell out a common word that either starts with S H or T H or ends with S H or S T. Find all the words as quickly as you can.

B E E H R T Y

C E N O S T T

A B B M O S T

D H I L L S U

A H I N R S T

E F H L S T Y

A E H K P S U

A C E H L L S

Add an M to each of the words below and then rearrange the letters in each word to form a new seven-letter word.

Each of the four-letter groups below may be extended on both the right and the left to form an eight-letter word. Drawing from the tiles directly above each group, fill in the blanks to find the words as quickly as you can.

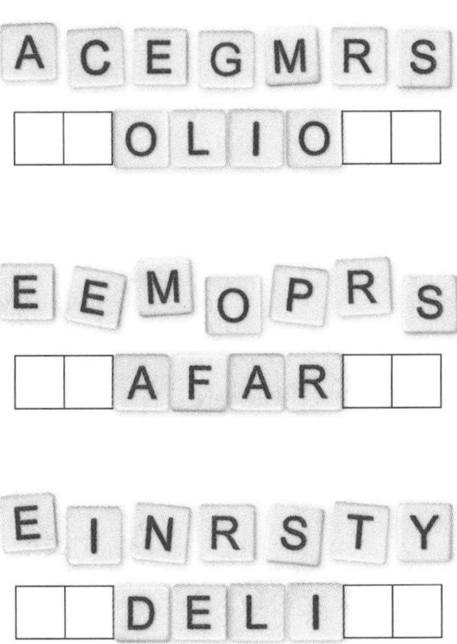

BANANA LEAVES

LEVEL

In each puzzle, use four of the tiles from the bunch to fill in the blanks and make an eight-letter word that connects the grid.

A E C M P S T

	☐		
W	H	E	N
	☐		
T	R	A	Y
	☐		
C	A	B	
	☐		
H	Y	P	E

	☐			
C	H	E	W	
	☐			
U	N	T	O	
	☐			
A	H	E	A	D
	☐			
V	I	E	W	

A C A E G S T

Each set of letters is arranged alphabetically. The ? is in the correct alphabetical position. Figure out what letter the ? represents and rearrange the letters to spell a seven-letter word that begins with the given letter. For example, in AAIN?TV the ? could be an N, O, P, Q, R, S, or T. Here it represents an R, which can be combined with the other letters to spell VARIANT.

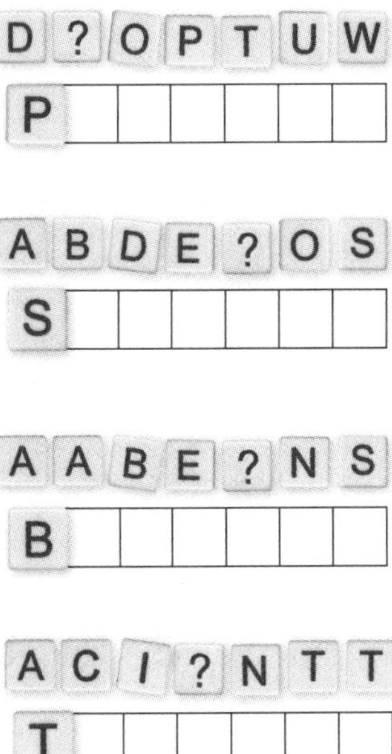

There is one letter that when added to all of the six-letter words below can be used to form new seven-letter words. Find the letter that works for all four words, add it to each word, and then rearrange each set of letters to form a new word. For example, B can be added to LOSS, ONLY, AUTO, and IRON to form SLOBS, NOBLY, ABOUT, and ROBIN.

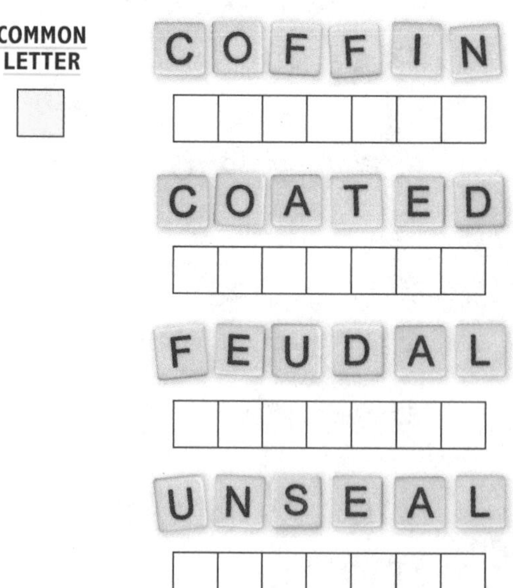

TOTALLY BANANAS

For each of the words below, replace one letter with the tile after the plus sign. Then rearrange the letters to spell a type of animal.

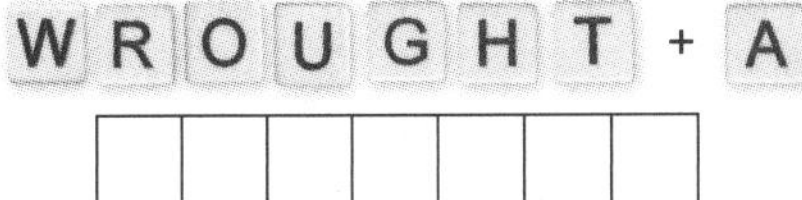

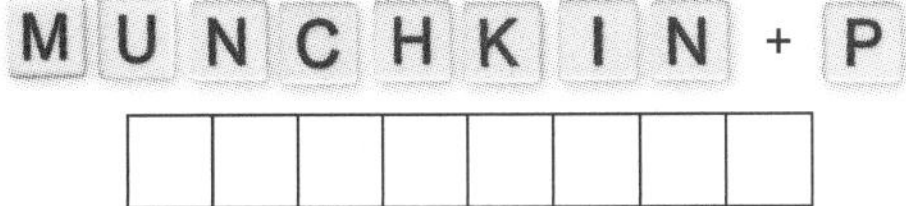

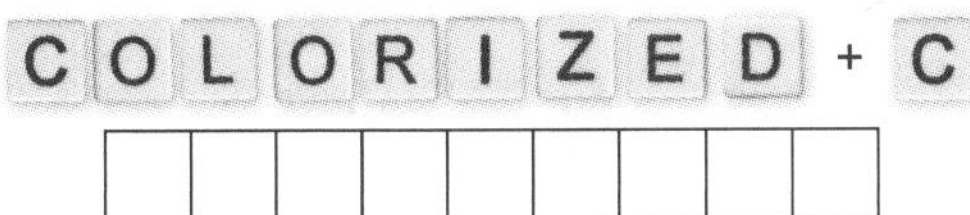

FRIED BANANAS

LEVEL

Rearrange the tiles below to spell a seven-letter word that fits in the first row. Then drop one letter and rearrange the remaining tiles to spell a six-letter word in the next row. Continue dropping one letter until you complete all six words. To get you started, one tile has been placed in each row.

A C N O O R T

_ A _ _ _ _ _

_ _ C _ _ _

_ C _ _ _

R _ _ _

N _ _

_ N

Using each four- and three-letter word just once, combine a word in the left column with a word in the right column. Then rearrange each seven-letter scramble to form a word that begins with a T, P, or C and write it into the appropriate space below.

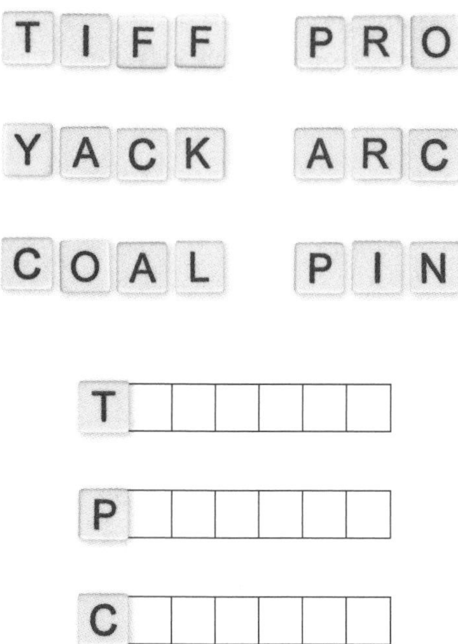

For the word group below, change one letter in the top word to one of the letters that appears in the bottom word, then rearrange the tiles to form a new common word. Do the same with each new word until you arrive at the bottom word.

For example, one path from BARK to PLUM is BARK, MARK, RAMP, RUMP, PLUM.

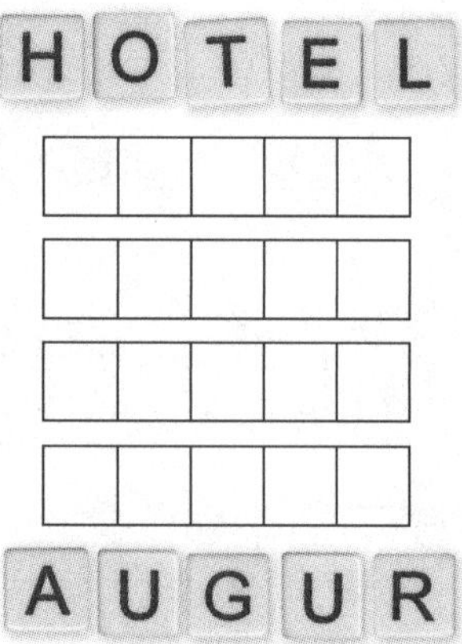

BUNCH OF BANANAS

LEVEL

For each word or phrase below, rearrange the letters to spell two types of weapons. For example, DRAW SPORES can be rearranged to spell SWORD, SPEAR.

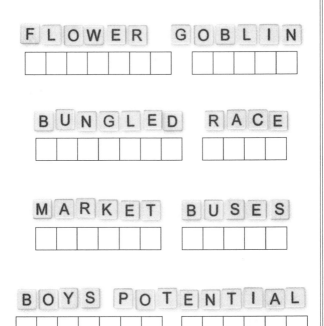

F L O W E R G O B L I N

B U N G L E D R A C E

M A R K E T B U S E S

B O Y S P O T E N T I A L

For each bunch below, rearrange the letters to form two intersecting words that fit into the corresponding grid.

A B C D L L M N P U U

A A A B I I O R R W Y

Each of the words below can be turned into another word on the list by changing one letter and then rearranging them all to form a new word. For example, REGIMENT can be turned into STEERING by changing the M to an S, so they would be a pair. How quickly can you find all the pairs?

1. F R O G M A N
2. F L O T S A M
3. G R A Y O U T
4. L A G O O N S
5. Y O G H U R T
6. G O R M A N D
7. M A L T O S E
8. G A S O H O L

Pairs

___	___
___	___
___	___
___	___

Each set of 12 tiles contains two common six-letter words. The letters of the first six-letter word are adjacent, but not in order. Find them and rearrange them to spell a word. Cross out those letters and rearrange the six remaining letters to spell the second word.

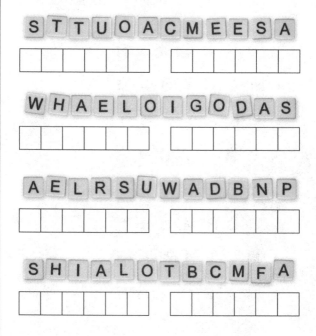

S T T U O A C M E E S A

W H A E L O I G O D A S

A E L R S U W A D B N P

S H I A L O T B C M F A

Rearrange the letters of each word below and place them in the blanks so that, together with the two letters that have already been placed, they form a new word.

Use the 15 tiles in this bunch to create words that fit into the grids below. To get you started, a few tiles from the bunch have been placed in the grid. Reuse the 15 tiles in the bunch for each grid.

C A I L T I T

D G N S I L U V

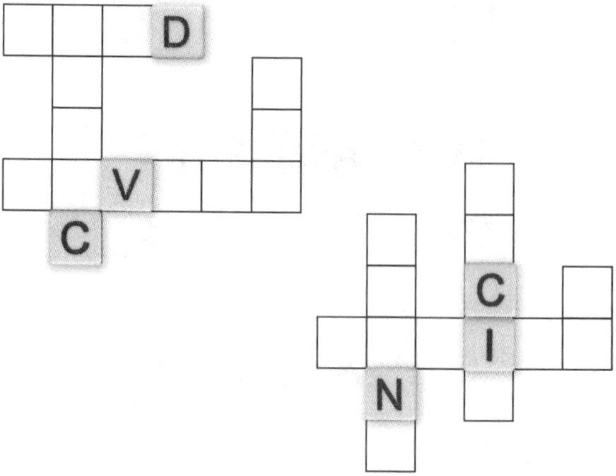

D

V

C

C

I

N

Each of the following seven-letter sets can be rearranged to spell out a common word that either starts with C H or R E or ends with A L or L E. Find all the words as quickly as you can.

A A G L R S T

A C E L N R T

A E E F M R R

C C E I L T U

A C D E H I R

A C C H I O T

A B D E L R U

C E E E I R V

Add an H to each of the words below and then rearrange the letters in each word to form a new seven-letter word.

Each of the four-letter groups below may be extended on both the right and the left to form an eight-letter word. Drawing from the tiles directly above each group, fill in the blanks to find the words as quickly as you can.

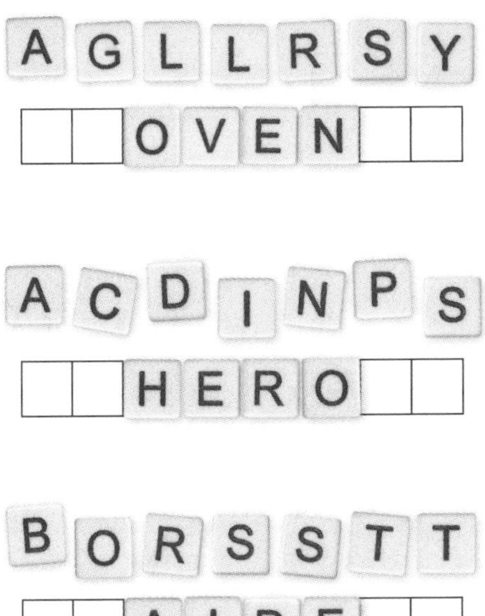

BANANA LEAVES

In each puzzle, use four of the tiles from the bunch to fill in the blanks and make an eight-letter word that connects the grid.

E I H N N R T

PATH
AGAIN
MARK
CLUE

WAVY
SIGN
CHIN
BLEND

L M M P R S T

Each set of letters is arranged alphabetically. The ? is in the correct alphabetical position. Figure out what letter the ? represents and rearrange the letters to spell a seven-letter word that begins with the given letter. For example, in AAIN?TV the ? could be an N, O, P, Q, R, S, or T. Here it represents an R, which can be combined with the other letters to spell VARIANT.

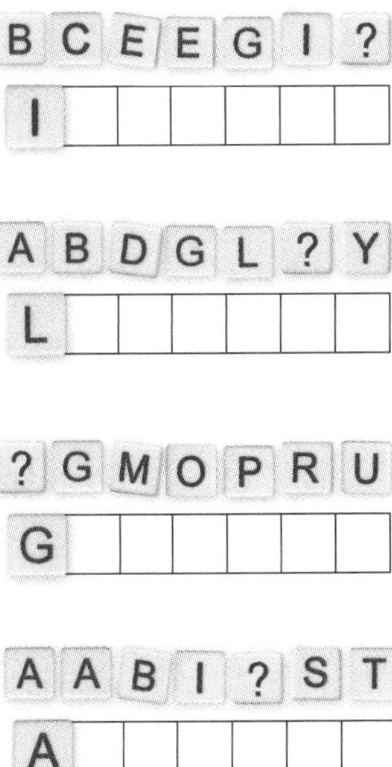

There is one letter that when added to all of the six-letter words below can be used to form new seven-letter words. Find the letter that works for all four words, add it to each word, and then rearrange each set of letters to form a new word. For example, B can be added to LOSS, ONLY, AUTO, and IRON to form SLOBS, NOBLY, ABOUT, and ROBIN.

COMMON LETTER

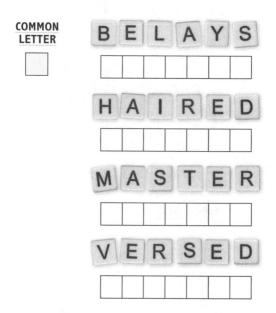

B E L A Y S

H A I R E D

M A S T E R

V E R S E D

LEVEL

For each of the words below, replace one letter with the tile after the plus sign. Then rearrange the letters to spell something people take to the beach.

U N C L O A K S + B

D E R B I E S + F

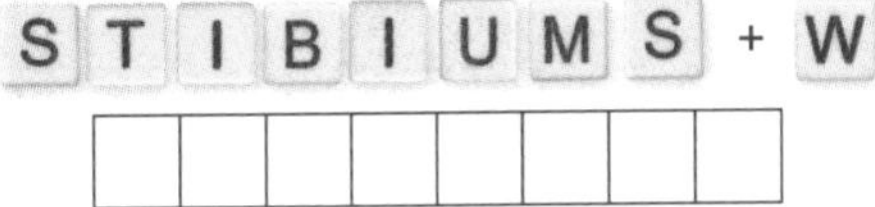

Rearrange the tiles below to spell a seven-letter word that fits in the first row. Then drop one letter and rearrange the remaining tiles to spell a six-letter word in the next row. Continue dropping one letter until you complete all six words. To get you started, one tile has been placed in each row.

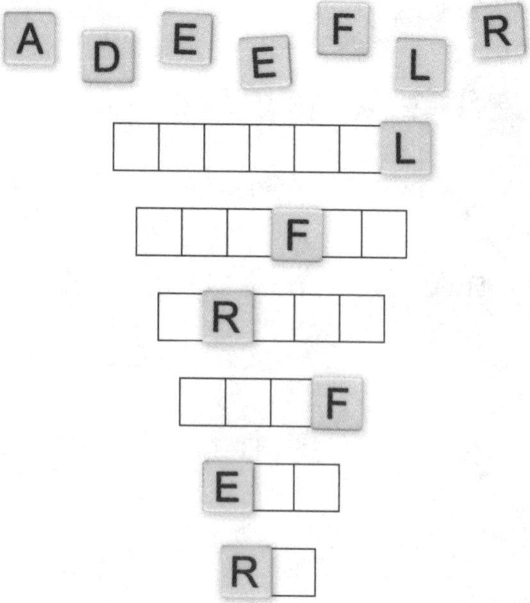

A D E E F L R

						L

			F		

	R			

			F

E		

R	

Using each four- and three-letter word just once, combine a word in the left column with a word in the right column. Then rearrange each seven-letter scramble to form a word that begins with an E, P, or O and write it into the appropriate space below.

RARE	MUD
PEER	HAT
TIRE	DUO

E _ _ _ _ _ _

P _ _ _ _ _ _

O _ _ _ _ _ _

For the word group below, change one letter in the top word to one of the letters that appears in the bottom word, then rearrange the tiles to form a new common word. Do the same with each new word until you arrive at the bottom word.

For example, one path from BARK to PLUM is BARK, MARK, RAMP, RUMP, PLUM.

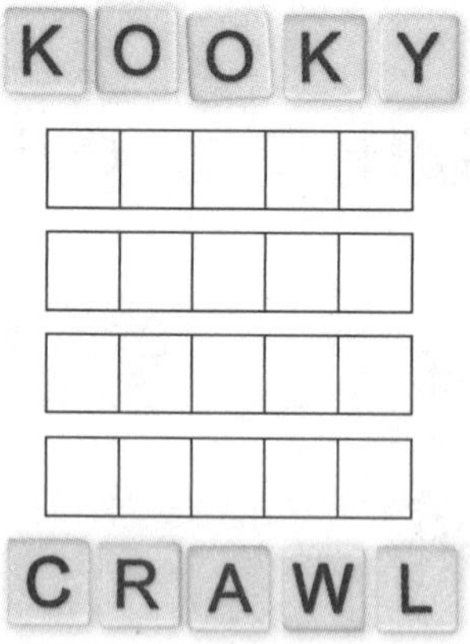

BUNCH OF BANANAS

For each word or phrase below, rearrange the letters to spell two things that are either a fruit or a vegetable. For example, CREEPY LAPEL can be rearranged to spell APPLE, CELERY.

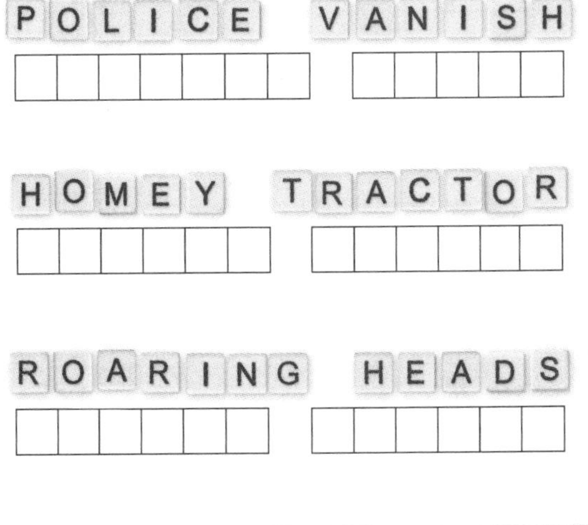

For each bunch below, rearrange the letters to form two intersecting words that fit into the corresponding grid.

A A C C I I N T N U Y

A B C I C G I R M T T

Each of the words below can be turned into another word on the list by changing one letter and then rearranging them all to form a new word. For example, REGIMENT can be turned into STEERING by changing the M to an S, so they would be a pair. How quickly can you find all the pairs?

1. O B L I G E D
2. D I S R O B E
3. G O D L I K E
4. O N E T I M E
5. I G N O B L E
6. A B I D E R S
7. E B O N I T E
8. B E G O N I A

Pairs

____ ____

____ ____

____ ____

____ ____

Each set of 12 tiles contains two common six-letter words. The letters of the first six-letter word are adjacent, but not in order. Find them and rearrange them to spell a word. Cross out those letters and rearrange the six remaining letters to spell the second word.

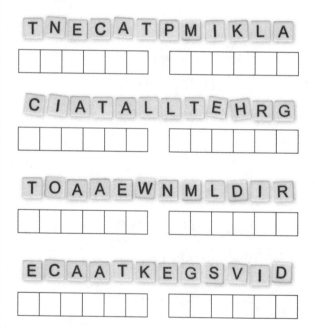

T N E C A T P M I K L A

C I A T A L L T E H R G

T O A A E W N M L D I R

E C A A T K E G S V I D

Rearrange the letters of each word below and place them in the blanks so that, together with the two letters that have already been placed, they form a new word.

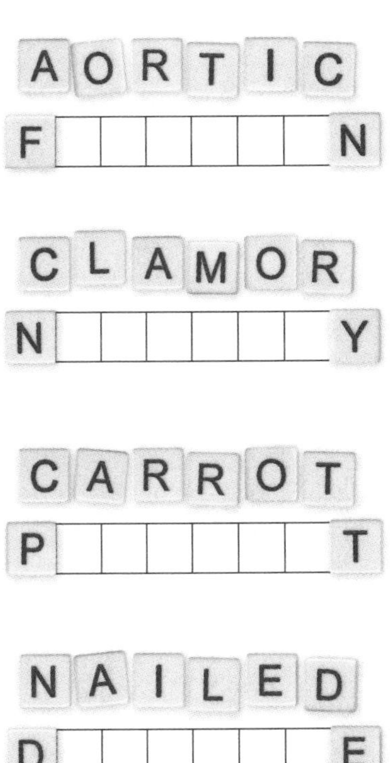

Use the 15 tiles in this bunch to create words that fit into the grids below. To get you started, a few tiles from the bunch have been placed in the grid. Reuse the 15 tiles in the bunch for each grid.

D A J I E N X

H F D M E O Y O

Each of the following seven-letter sets can be rearranged to spell out a common word that either starts with S L or T H or ends with N E or O R. Find all the words as quickly as you can.

A A D O P R T

E G H I L S T

A A B E L N O

A G L N O R U

E L O S S T W

C E G L N O O

C E H I K T T

B E E H R T Y

Add an N to each of the words below and then rearrange the letters in each word to form a new seven-letter word.

Each of the four-letter groups below may be extended on both the right and the left to form an eight-letter word. Drawing from the tiles directly above each group, fill in the blanks to find the words as quickly as you can.

BANANA LEAVES

In each puzzle, use four of the tiles from the bunch to fill in the blanks and make an eight-letter word that connects the grid.

B L C M R T V

		☐		
S	H	A	P	E
		☐		
	L	A	U	G	H
		☐		
	H	O	P	E
		☐		
	B	Y	T	E

	☐		
F	O	A	L
	☐		
C	E	N	T
	☐		
I	D	O	L
	☐		
T	W	I	N

B H E L N R Y

Each set of letters is arranged alphabetically. The ? is in the correct alphabetical position. Figure out what letter the ? represents and rearrange the letters to spell a seven-letter word that begins with the given letter. For example, in AAIN?TV the ? could be an N, O, P, Q, R, S, or T. Here it represents an R, which can be combined with the other letters to spell VARIANT.

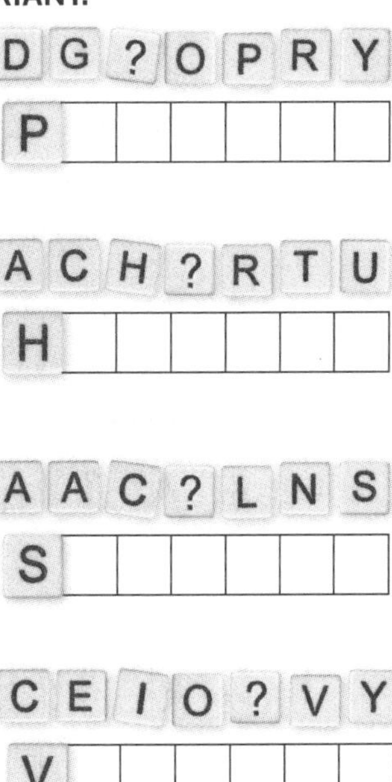

There is one letter that when added to all of the six-letter words below can be used to form new seven-letter words. Find the letter that works for all four words, add it to each word, and then rearrange each set of letters to form a new word. For example, B can be added to LOSS, ONLY, AUTO, and IRON to form SLOBS, NOBLY, ABOUT, and ROBIN.

COMMON LETTER

T H R E E S

H A T R E D

H E A T E R

I N M A T E

For each of the words below, replace one letter with the tile after the plus sign. Then rearrange the letters to spell a chemical element.

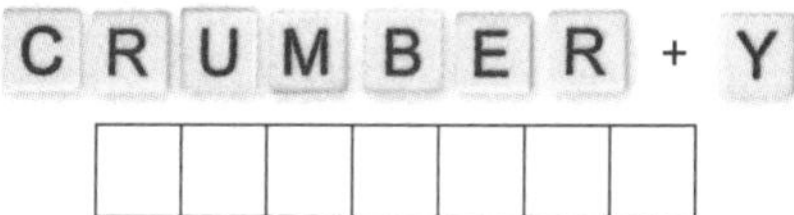

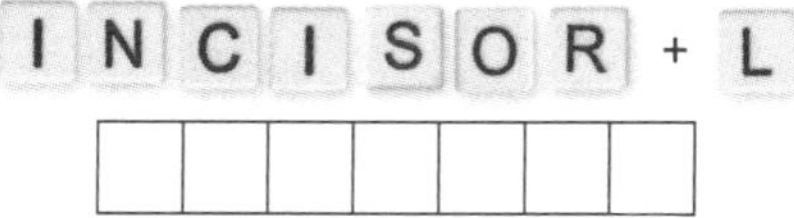

Rearrange the tiles below to spell a seven-letter word that fits in the first row. Then drop one letter and rearrange the remaining tiles to spell a six-letter word in the next row. Continue dropping one letter until you complete all six words. To get you started, one tile has been placed in each row.

A D G L N O Y

		Y				

			G		

			N	

D			

	N	

	N

Using each four- and three-letter word just once, combine a word in the left column with a word in the right column. Then rearrange each seven-letter scramble to form a word that begins with an A, F, or P and write it into the appropriate space below.

For the word group below, change one letter in the top word to one of the letters that appears in the bottom word, then rearrange the tiles to form a new common word. Do the same with each new word until you arrive at the bottom word.

For example, one path from BARK to PLUM is BARK, MARK, RAMP, RUMP, PLUM.

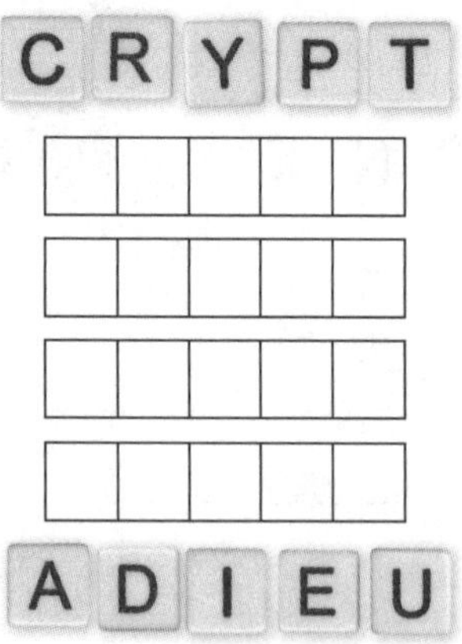

BUNCH OF BANANAS

For each word or phrase below, rearrange the letters to spell two things that are sweet treats. For example, LIMB PLAGUE can be rearranged to spell PIE, GUMBALL.

CROC LIFE GUIDE

TRY HERB PASTES

CUPID PACKED GUN

A DITSY CRANIUM

For each bunch below, rearrange the letters to form two intersecting words that fit into the corresponding grid.

A A L L M N S U N U Y

C A L O N N R T Y T X

Each of the words below can be turned into another word on the list by changing one letter and then rearranging them all to form a new word. For example, REGIMENT can be turned into STEERING by changing the M to an S, so they would be a pair. How quickly can you find all the pairs?

1. SECEDES
2. UNACTED
3. POLICED
4. ESSENCE
5. DEFICIT
6. COLLIDE
7. DEFUNCT
8. EIDETIC

Pairs

___ ___

___ ___

___ ___

___ ___

LEVEL

Each set of 12 tiles contains two common six-letter words. The letters of the first six-letter word are adjacent, but not in order. Find them and rearrange them to spell a word. Cross out those letters and rearrange the six remaining letters to spell the second word.

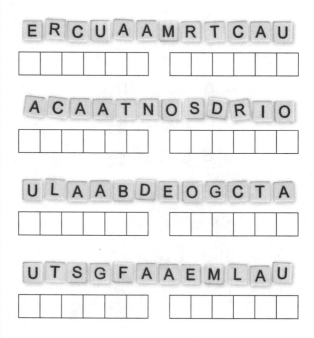

E R C U A A M R T C A U

A C A A T N O S D R I O

U L A A B D E O G C T A

U T S G F A A E M L A U

Rearrange the letters of each word below and place them in the blanks so that, together with the two letters that have already been placed, they form a new word.

Use the 15 tiles in this bunch to create words that fit into the grids below. To get you started, a few tiles from the bunch have been placed in the grid. Reuse the 15 tiles in the bunch for each grid.

R N I S Y R P

D A O R T I R B

N I S D B Y

LEVEL

Each of the following seven-letter sets can be rearranged to spell out a common word that either starts with CR or DR or ends with ID or TY. Find all the words as quickly as you can.

A C L R S T Y

A B C O R R W

A C F L T U Y

A D I I L N V

A A D I L W Y

A D I L T U Y

A D E P R R Y

D E L O P R T

Add a D to each of the words below and then rearrange the letters in each word to form a new seven-letter word.

Each of the four-letter groups below may be extended on both the right and the left to form an eight-letter word. Drawing from the tiles directly above each group, fill in the blanks to find the words as quickly as you can.

In each puzzle, use four of the tiles from the bunch to fill in the blanks and make an eight-letter word that connects the grid.

A R D H I B E

_ REAP _ COAST _ VEAL _ QAT

_ HOME _ WHET _ LUNG _ FEED

C L D T R L M

BANANA CHIPS

LEVEL

Each set of letters is arranged alphabetically. The ? is in the correct alphabetical position. Figure out what letter the ? represents and rearrange the letters to spell a seven-letter word that begins with the given letter. For example, in AAIN?TV the ? could be an N, O, P, Q, R, S, or T. Here it represents an R, which can be combined with the other letters to spell VARIANT.

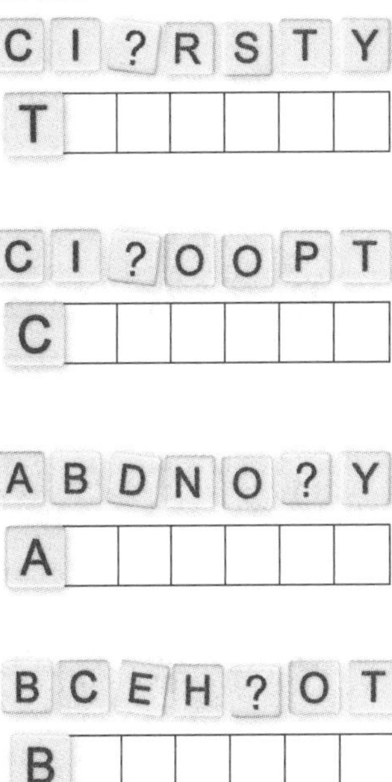

BANANA PEELS

There is one letter that when added to all of the six-letter words below can be used to form new seven-letter words. Find the letter that works for all four words, add it to each word, and then rearrange each set of letters to form a new word. For example, B can be added to LOSS, ONLY, AUTO, and IRON to form SLOBS, NOBLY, ABOUT, and ROBIN.

COMMON LETTER

R A T T E D

P E A H E N

U P T E A R

Y E A S T S

TOTALLY BANANAS

For each of the words below, replace one letter with the tile after the plus sign. Then rearrange the letters to spell a profession.

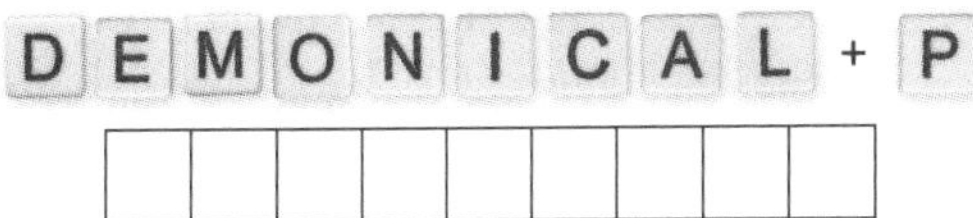

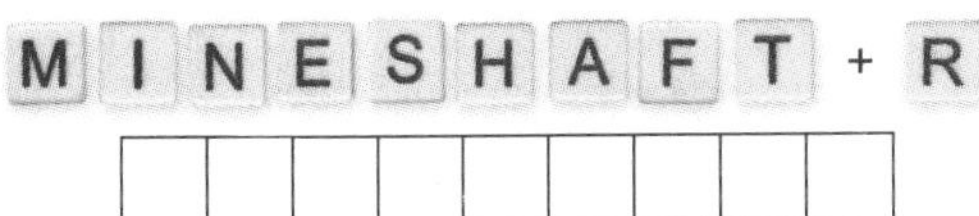

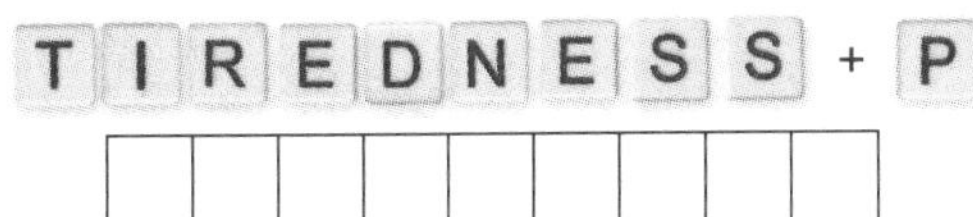

Rearrange the tiles below to spell a seven-letter word that fits in the first row. Then drop one letter and rearrange the remaining tiles to spell a six-letter word in the next row. Continue dropping one letter until you complete all six words. To get you started, one tile has been placed in each row.

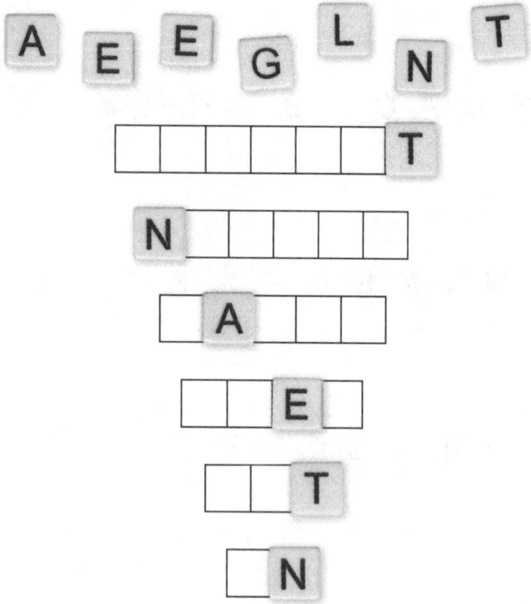

A E E G L N T

						T

N					

	A			

		E	

		T

	N

Using each four- and three-letter word just once, combine a word in the left column with a word in the right column. Then rearrange each seven-letter scramble to form a word that begins with a G, R, or H and write it into the appropriate space below.

DRUG	ERG
EVEN	MOP
HIRE	ONE

G _ _ _ _ _ _

R _ _ _ _ _ _

H _ _ _ _ _ _

For the word group below, change one letter in the top word to one of the letters that appears in the bottom word, then rearrange the tiles to form a new common word. Do the same with each new word until you arrive at the bottom word.

For example, one path from BARK to PLUM is BARK, MARK, RAMP, RUMP, PLUM.

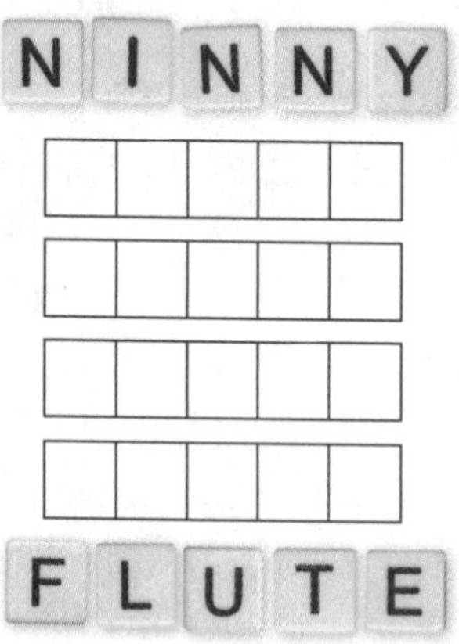

BUNCH OF BANANAS

For each word or phrase below, rearrange the letters to spell the last names of two well-known U.S. sports figures. For example, HUGER GIRTH can be rearranged to spell Babe RUTH, Lou GEHRIG.

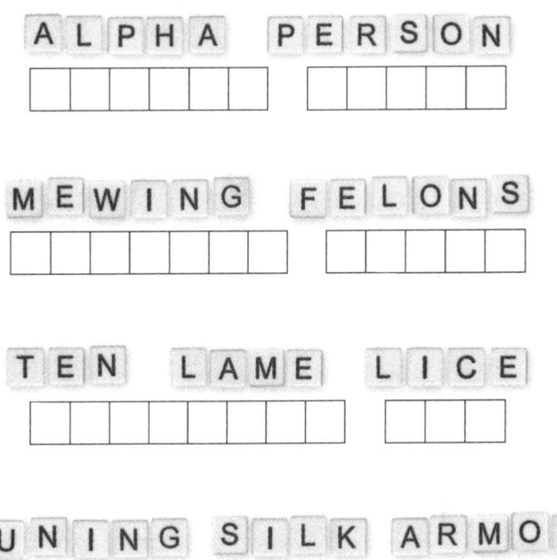

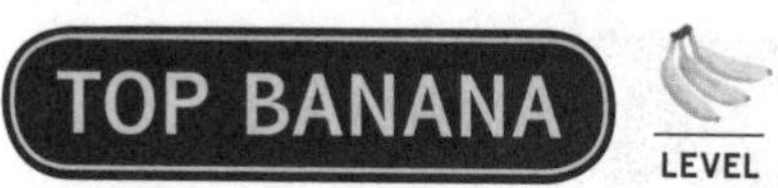

For each bunch below, rearrange the letters to form two intersecting words that fit into the corresponding grid.

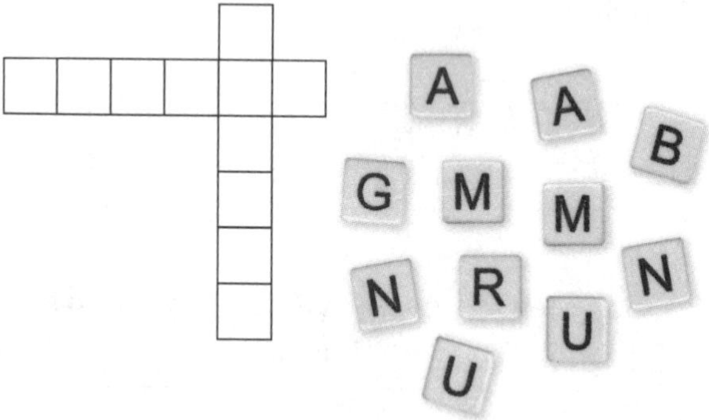

A A B G M M N R N U U

A A C I F F I P O S Y

Each of the words below can be turned into another word on the list by changing one letter and then rearranging them all to form a new word. For example, REGIMENT can be turned into STEERING by changing the M to an S, so they would be a pair. How quickly can you find all the pairs?

1. D I C T I O N
2. A C H I E S T
3. S O L I C I T
4. N O T I C E D
5. E C L I P S E
6. C H E M I S T
7. I C E L E S S
8. I T A L I C S

Pairs

___ ___

___ ___

___ ___

___ ___

LEVEL

Each set of 12 tiles contains two common six-letter words. The letters of the first six-letter word are adjacent, but not in order. Find them and rearrange them to spell a word. Cross out those letters and rearrange the six remaining letters to spell the second word.

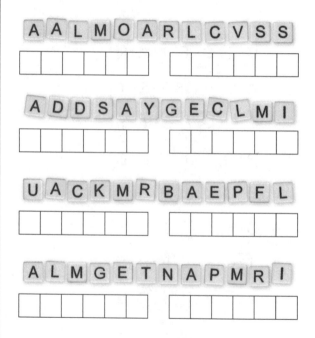

A A L M O A R L C V S S

A D D S A Y G E C L M I

U A C K M R B A E P F L

A L M G E T N A P M R I

Rearrange the letters of each word below and place them in the blanks so that, together with the two letters that have already been placed, they form a new word.

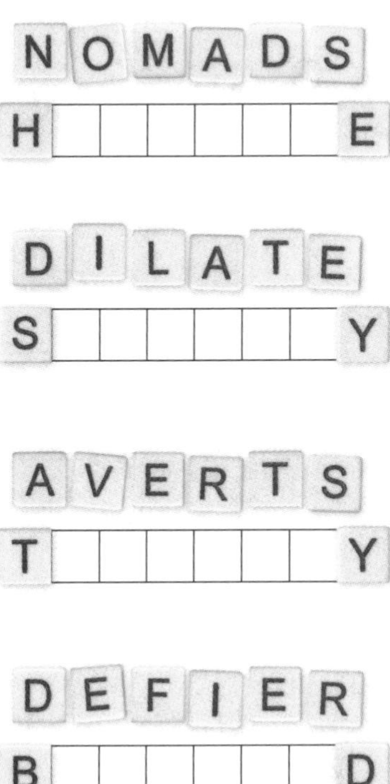

Use the 15 tiles in this bunch to create words that fit into the grids below. To get you started, a few tiles from the bunch have been placed in the grid. Reuse the 15 tiles in the bunch for each grid.

K E O N E W U

A L K E T E N E

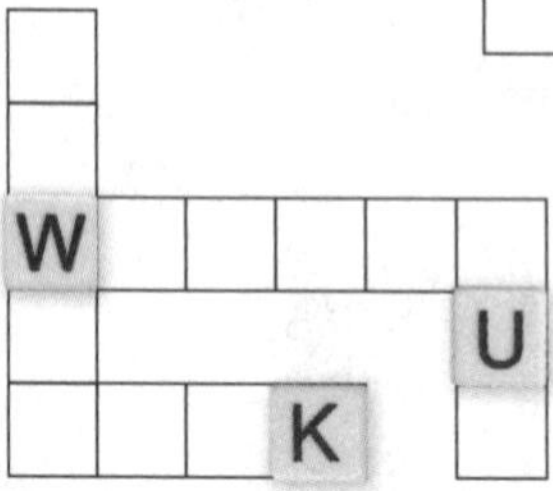

Each of the following seven-letter sets can be rearranged to spell out a common word that either starts with G R or B L and/or ends with E R or N E. Find all the words as quickly as you can.

A A C D E R V

A F G I R T Y

B E L N R T U

E F N O R T U

A E E H M N T

C E F I M O R

A E G L N R U

B L M O O S S

Add a G to each of the words below and then rearrange the letters in each word to form a new seven-letter word.

BANANA PUDDING

Each of the four-letter groups below may be extended on both the right and the left to form an eight-letter word. Drawing from the tiles directly above each group, fill in the blanks to find the words as quickly as you can.

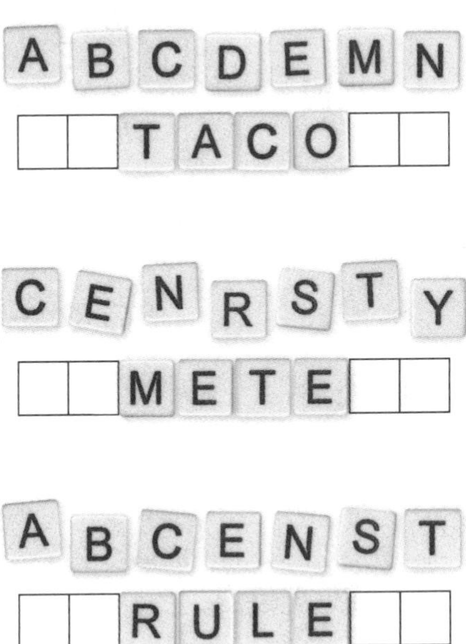

In each puzzle, use four of the tiles from the bunch to fill in the blanks and make an eight-letter word that connects the grid.

D I F L N R T

☐
MOUND
☐
FETCH
☐
BISON
☐
OCHER

☐
MICE
☐
BIKED
☐
TOTAL
☐
IMP

C N L O R S T

Each set of letters is arranged alphabetically. The ? is in the correct alphabetical position. Figure out what letter the ? represents and rearrange the letters to spell a seven-letter word that begins with the given letter. For example, in AAIN?TV the ? could be an N, O, P, Q, R, S, or T. Here it represents an R, which can be combined with the other letters to spell VARIANT.

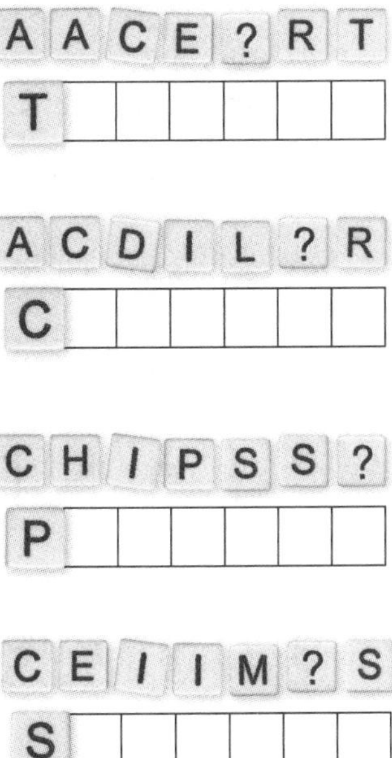

There is one letter that when added to all of the six-letter words below can be used to form new seven-letter words. Find the letter that works for all four words, add it to each word, and then rearrange each set of letters to form a new word. For example, B can be added to LOSS, ONLY, AUTO, and IRON to form SLOBS, NOBLY, ABOUT, and ROBIN.

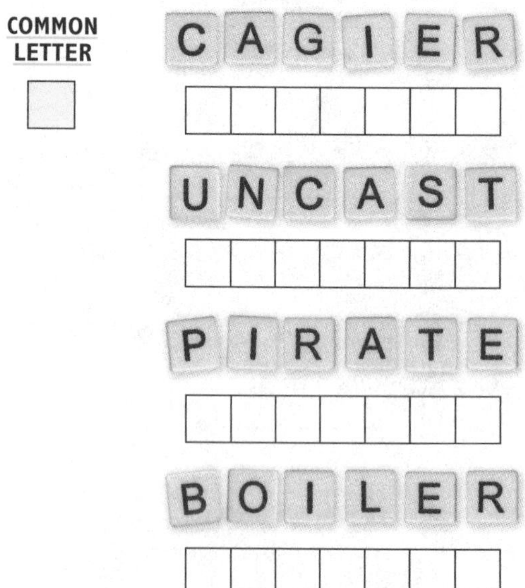

For each of the words below, replace one letter with the tile after the plus sign. Then rearrange the letters to spell something that is dangerous to touch.

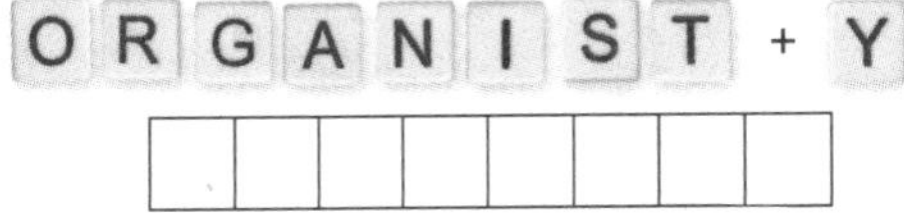

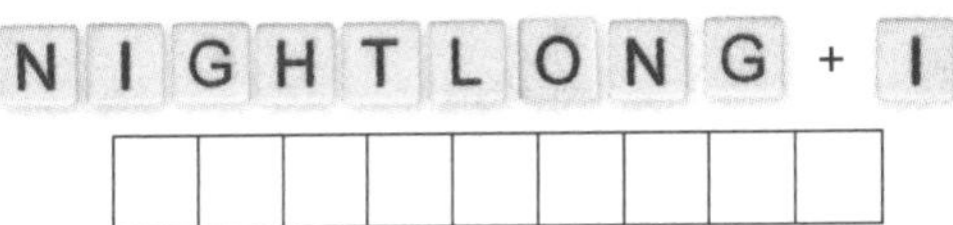

Rearrange the tiles below to spell a seven-letter word that fits in the first row. Then drop one letter and rearrange the remaining tiles to spell a six-letter word in the next row. Continue dropping one letter until you complete all six words. To get you started, one tile has been placed in each row.

E E F H O R T

	H					

				T	

E				

T			

	H	

	H

Using each four- and three-letter word just once, combine a word in the left column with a word in the right column. Then rearrange each seven-letter scramble to form a word that begins with an E, U, or H and write it into the appropriate space below.

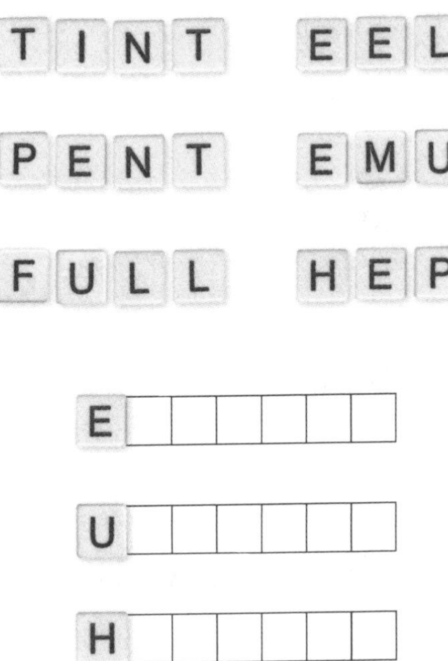

For the word group below, change one letter in the top word to one of the letters that appears in the bottom word, then rearrange the tiles to form a new common word. Do the same with each new word until you arrive at the bottom word.

For example, one path from BARK to PLUM is BARK, MARK, RAMP, RUMP, PLUM.

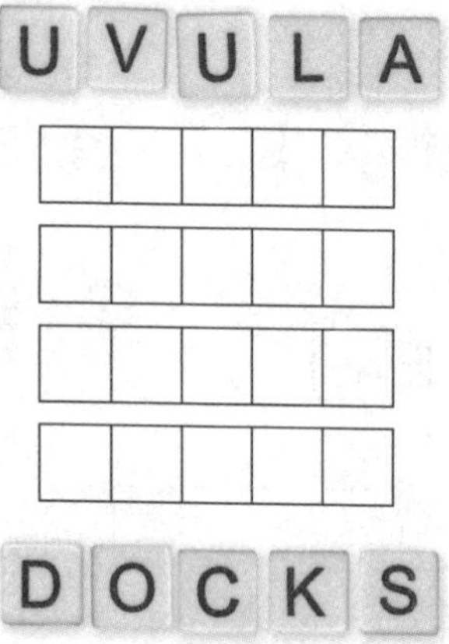

BUNCH OF BANANAS

For each word or phrase below, rearrange the letters to spell the last names of two comedians. For example, YACHT PROLES can be rearranged to spell Billy CRYSTAL, Bob HOPE.

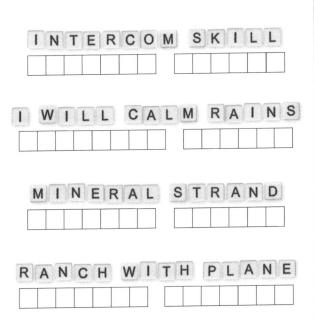

INTERCOM SKILL

I WILL CALM RAINS

MINERAL STRAND

RANCH WITH PLANE

ANSWER KEY

PAGE 18
HOWL, HOLE, LONE, OMEN, MEAN; HAIL, PAIL, LIMP, LUMP, JUMP

PAGE 19
TAR, SOOT; ANT, PUPIL; CROW, COAL; PANTHER, INK

PAGE 20

PAGE 21
1–3; 2–4; 5–7; 6–8

PAGE 22
ANNUL, LOGIC; TURBO, GRIEF; UNPEN, LYRIC; TRAWL, GOURD

PAGE 23
ARMADA, CANOLA, BEFALL, MARINA

PAGE 24

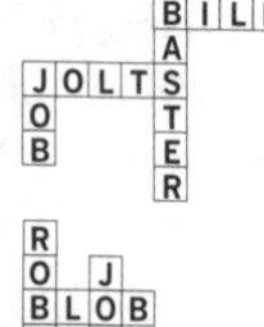

PAGE 25
BRAVER, LOCALE, GYRATE, CRAYON, RACIAL, SALUTE, BROACH, DRYISH

PAGE 26
DETACH, PARDON, BLONDE, CINDER

PAGE 27
HUMANE, RETOLD, WIDELY

PAGE 28
AROUND, HIATUS

PAGE 29
ENIGMA, APATHY, BISTRO, SEWAGE

PAGE 30
M: MOUTH, METRO, DIMLY, THYME

PAGE 31
BANKER, LAWYER, GROCER, PILOT

PAGE 32
BATON, BOAT, TAB, AT

PAGE 33
ALOOF, ENACT, LAPEL

PAGE 34
VICE, DICE, DIME, MODE, MOOD; ONCE, OMEN, MORN, DORM, DRUM

PAGE 35
EPIC, GRAND; SUPER, LARGE; HUGE, GIANT; VAST, GREAT

PAGE 36

PAGE 37
1–8; 2–4; 3–7; 5–6

PAGE 38
ASKED, APHID; PAUSE, PAYEE; COCOA, IMAGE; BEVEL, DOUGH

PAGE 39
BATBOY, BEDPAN, ANALOG, BREATH

PAGE 40

PAGE 41
CHERUB, IMBUED, ENROLL, GLADLY, CHEESY, DEBONE, MUMBLY, LEGEND

PAGE 42
DRAGON, TARGET, NAUGHT, FRIDGE

PAGE 43
STANZA, HEIFER, PAUPER

PAGE 44
HANSOM, VACUUM

PAGE 45
UPWARD, MARINA, DISUSE, CHOICE

PAGE 46
P: INPUT, ERUPT, PRAWN, PRISS

PAGE 47
GUARD, DEFENSE, CENTER, BLOCK

PAGE 48
PLACE, PLEA, PAL, PA

PAGE 49
BROIL, GAUNT, HUMID

PAGE 50
TURN, TRUE, ROTE, TOME, SOME; HALF, HALO, OPAL, ATOP, PORT

PAGE 51
BEN, STU; JAMES, RON; BOB, LEON; BILL, DAVE

PAGE 52

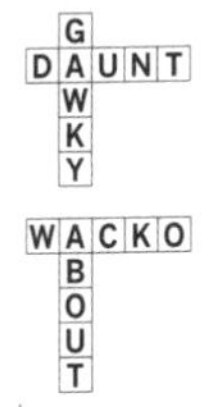

PAGE 53
1–4; 2–7; 3–5; 6–8

PAGE 54
CREPT, BUTTE; OFTEN, VAULT; FOYER, BUILT; RADAR, OCTET

PAGE 55
BARREL, ABRUPT, UNCLAD, HEPCAT

PAGE 56

PAGE 57
BIDDEN, GROUND, OCTANE, VANITY, THRIVE, GRISLY, IODINE, COBALT

PAGE 58
ABSENT, MENTOR, TONSIL, TAVERN

PAGE 59
FIERCE, PAGODA, ALBEIT

PAGE 60
LOATHE, EUREKA

PAGE 61
TARTAR, YELPED, STATIC, ASTRAY

PAGE 62
W: TWERP, SHREW, TWEEN, FEWER

PAGE 63
SMILE, LIGHT, IDEAS, FLAME

PAGE 64
CHINA, CHAI, CHI, HI

PAGE 65
SCOUT, WHEAT, YOUTH

PAGE 66
GRIN, REIN, SINE, SEEN, EYES; ZINC, COIN, OINK, KNOW, WORK

PAGE 67
SHARP, FLAT; RICH, POOR; SIT, STAND; HEAD, TAIL

PAGE 68

PAGE 69
1–6; 2–5; 3–7; 4–8

PAGE 70
RERAN, ALOHA; SWAMI, SAUNA; OMEGA, THETA; GRAFT, LAUGH

PAGE 71
ANEMIC, FACTOR, SOCIAL, CATNIP

PAGE 72

PAGE 73
BEACON, TURBAN, HEALTH, MATRON, INTACT, INVERT, GLITCH HIDDEN

PAGE 74
AMORAL, GARBLE, HERALD, ANKLET

PAGE 75
MOHAWK, BIKINI, AFLOAT

PAGE 76
ADRIFT, THROAT

PAGE 77
ORDAIN, MARGIN, THRICE, SALARY

PAGE 78
H: MIRTH, BUSHY, OUGHT, FIGHT

PAGE 79
SPHERE, DONUT, CONE, HELIX

PAGE 80
HYENA, YEAH, YEA, AY

PAGE 81
FOLIO, REUSE, TWEEN

PAGE 82
HOPE, OPEN, PINE, PINT, UNIT; FLAX, AXLE, ZEAL, HAZE, CHEZ

PAGE 83
DINGHY, BOAT; CANOE, KAYAK; SHIP, YACHT; RAFT, FERRY

PAGE 84

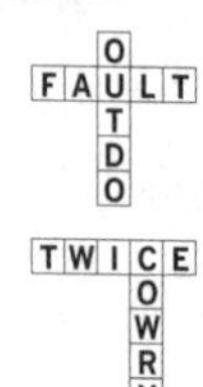

PAGE 85
1–7; 2–4; 3–6; 5–8

PAGE 86
BATIK, PIECE;
OGLER, BATHE;
BOGUS, HAZEL;
FRANC, BEGUN

PAGE 87
DEFLEA, ADHERE,
AGEDLY, HERALD

PAGE 88

PAGE 89
LACKEY, LAGOON,
VOIDED, IMPALE,
BEHELD, FABLED,
KNOWER, GARLIC

PAGE 90
SOARER, HOORAY,
SPIRAL, CHROME

PAGE 91
DOMINO, TUMULT,
BINARY

PAGE 92
UNEASY, POPLAR

PAGE 93
VEILED, ABDUCT,
DOODAD, RADIUS

PAGE 94
F: MOTIF, FILTH,
FETID, FOLDS

PAGE 95
DAGGER, NEEDLE,
SWORD, TONGUE

PAGE 96
WOMEN, MEOW,
WOE, OW

PAGE 97
ADMIT, THUMB,
FAITH

PAGE 98
GOAL, LOAN, NAIL,
MAIN, MINK; WHEW,
WHEY, THEY, TYPE,
PITY

PAGE 99
ALIEN, PSYCHO;
LOLITA, CRASH;
GHOST, OLIVER;
TITANIC, FAME

PAGE 100

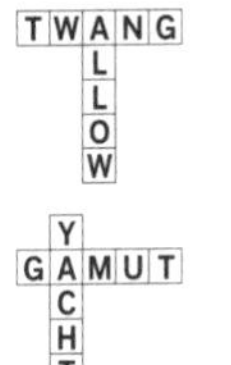

PAGE 101
1–5; 2–6; 3–8; 4–7

PAGE 102
ARMOR, HEATH;
WHOLE, BEGOT;
HYPER, PECAN;
CANAL, AGONY

PAGE 103
ALLUDE, STEADY,
SENATE, FIXATE

PAGE 104

PAGE 105
GATHER, FLORAL,
ABSURD, FLIMSY,
OUTDID, FROZEN,
UNPAID, MIDGET

PAGE 106
RANCID, CANYON,
DEPICT, CHOSEN

PAGE 107
LINEAR, BIOPSY,
CHORUS

PAGE 108
WEAPON, FORMAT

PAGE 109
BLEACH, COWARD, SELDOM, GAMBIT

PAGE 110
Y: IMPLY, MONEY, FOYER, ABYSM

PAGE 111
HANGAR, RUNWAY, TICKET, LUGGAGE

PAGE 112
THYME, THEM, MET, EM

PAGE 113
HEATH, LIBEL, BARON

PAGE 114
POLE, LODE, RODE, RIDE, GRID; JINX, JOIN, INFO, FOND, DOFF

PAGE 115
MONK, BOURNE; HOUSE, POTTER; HULK, SUPERMAN; SPOCK, DOROTHY

PAGE 116

PAGE 117
1–5; 2–4; 3–6; 7–8

PAGE 118
BEIGE, AUGUR; LAYUP, REBEL; APPLY, IMBUE; APRON, ROBOT

PAGE 119
GNAWER, VOYAGE, THREAT, MUTATE

PAGE 120

PAGE 121
DIVERT, REVERT, NOBODY, CUTEST, PLEDGE, PREYED, TYRANT, PROMPT

PAGE 122
MAGNET, STIGMA, WARMLY, MESHED

PAGE 123
BUSHEL, DISOWN, BOTANY

PAGE 124
UNSAFE, RAMROD

PAGE 125
INLAID, HUSTLE, LUNACY, BAGFUL

PAGE 126
C: COYER, MINCE, WENCH, SPICY

PAGE 127
NINE, EIGHTY, SEVEN, THREE

PAGE 128
VENOM, OVEN, ONE, EN

PAGE 129
BOUGH, GAVEL, HAIKU

PAGE 130
TYPE, POET, COPE, COOP, LOCO; PULP, PLUM, LAMP, LOAM, FOAM

PAGE 131
PEACE, SHOW; SPRING, MEAL; DINNER, LIFE; DOWN, SOME

PAGE 132

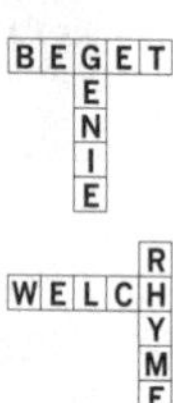

PAGE 133
1–5; 2–6; 3–7; 4–8

PAGE 134
WOMAN, BEFIT; BLOND, FOCUS; RATIO, CURVY; COMFY, ONION

PAGE 135
GLAMOR, HATPIN, BUSHEL, BISTRO

PAGE 136

PAGE 137
PALLOR, RECTOR, UNMADE, REMAKE, DEFACE, SPLICE, STIGMA, BETTOR

PAGE 138
INHALE, BEHOLD, THRIVE, MOTHER

PAGE 139
BLOWUP, APPEAR, CEREAL

PAGE 140
CRAYON, GOALIE

PAGE 141
FAUCET, PLACID, ABRUPT, ABOUND

PAGE 142
B: BONGO, BELLY, EMBED, BOSSY

PAGE 143
MENU, DISH, BOOTH, ENTRÉE

PAGE 144
LINEN, NINE, INN, IN

PAGE 145
MOUND, ADOPT, LAUGH

PAGE 146
PLAIN, ALIGN, GLINT, INGOT, THONG, TOUGH

PAGE 147
RUBY, GARNET; SLATE, DIAMOND; GRANITE, OPAL; MARBLE, AGATE

PAGE 148

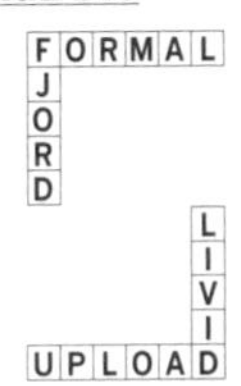

PAGE 149
1–4; 2–7; 3–6; 5–8

PAGE 150
ANNEX, HYENAS; GRAVY, GORGON; THANK, TIPTOP; VITAL, UNJUST

PAGE 151
HARPIST, INSULAR, UTOPIAN, TRANSIT

PAGE 152

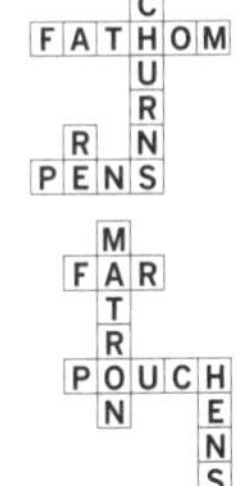

PAGE 153
CANDID, BOBCAT, GAWKED, BAITED, BANDIT, RABBIT, HEAVEN, ACCORD

PAGE 154
SCANDAL, ABSCOND, WAKENED, PLACARD

PAGE 155
TITANIC, DEFUNCT, STARTUP

PAGE 156
ARCHWAY, ACTUARY

PAGE 157
LEAGUE, CURFEW, WRAITH, GUFFAW

PAGE 158
F: FERVOR, MUFFLE, FLATLY, FISHED

PAGE 159
SCALE, SHOWER, FLOSS, TOWEL

PAGE 160
ATTAIN, TITAN, TINT, NIT, IN

PAGE 161
BADMAN, CAMERA, CANVAS

PAGE 162
RIDER, CIDER, CARED, REACH, ROACH, COACH

PAGE 163
SPEARS, DYLAN; GAGA, EMINEM; PRESLEY, DION; CHER, TWAIN

PAGE 164

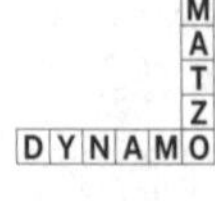

CAUCUS
UNDID

PAGE 165
1–5; 2–4; 3–7; 6–8

PAGE 166
PIANO, POISON; ROYAL, AIRBAG; BERRY, SULFUR; IDIOT, IMPISH

PAGE 167
REFRAIN, PAYROLL, MASONRY, AUTOPSY

PAGE 168

PAGE 169
INNATE, INWARD, VALUED, CAKIER, ACROSS, CAREER, EMBODY, DECEIT

PAGE 170
TWANGED, GRAVEST, TANGENT, SYRINGE

PAGE 171
MADONNA, ATLASES, GRANDPA

PAGE 172
WARHEAD, OFFBEAT

PAGE 173
HIATUS, IMPALE, TOUPEE, YEOMAN

PAGE 174
H: BROACH, HERBAL, GATHER, SHADOW

PAGE 175
HOUSE, PALACE, STABLE, PRISON

PAGE 176
ADVERB, RAVED, AVER, REV, ER

PAGE 177
APPEAR, CANARY, GARAGE

PAGE 178
FLOUR, FLORA, CORAL, CLEAR, LACED, CAKED

PAGE 179
DOE, PANTHER; HAMSTER, FLEA; GIRAFFE, ANT; CRANE, STORK

PAGE 180

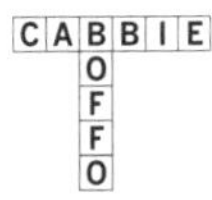

PAGE 181
1–6; 2–5; 3–7; 4–8

PAGE 182
CLEFT, SYRUPY; UNCUT, WISDOM; WIDTH, PHOOEY; ARROW, INKJET

PAGE 183
BUTCHER, OBSCURE, FORBODE, WEBSITE

PAGE 184

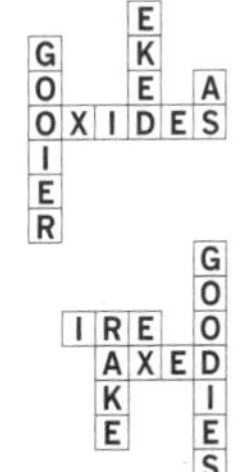

PAGE 185
MAYHEM, CANOLA, FAUCET, CANCEL, LIZARD, EMBLEM, LAVISH, HARBOR

PAGE 186
PATELLA, RECLUSE, CENTRAL, FRAILTY

PAGE 187
AGENDUM, LACONIC, AUDITED

PAGE 188
DELOUSE, GENUINE

PAGE 189
AWHILE, BUFFET, GUITAR, FIESTA

PAGE 190
W: SWERVE, SHREWD, RIPSAW, WEAPON

PAGE 191
SKIRT, KIMONO, SCARF, SWEATER

PAGE 192
EMBALM, LEMMA, MEAL, ELM, ME

PAGE 193
IMPALA, NAPALM, ABOUND

PAGE 194
ORBIT, RATIO, ACTOR, CORAL, CLOAK, SLACK

PAGE 195
FOOT, HAIR; HEART, NAIL; FOREHEAD, RIBS; TONSILS, CHEEK

PAGE 196

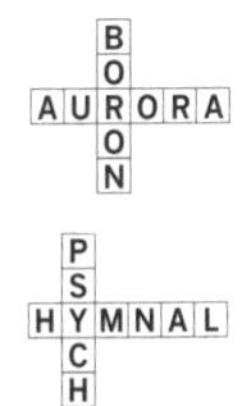

PAGE 197
1–7; 2–6; 3–5; 4–8

PAGE 198
NIECE, HONCHO; MICRO, FOLKSY; GUILD, MALADY; EPOCH, NOTIFY

PAGE 199
BLEMISH, BRISKET, LIBERTY, BREVITY

PAGE 200

PAGE 201
MANTRA, NINETY, NIBBLE, AIDING, OCCUPY, WARMTH, VULGAR, FENCER

PAGE 202
BARGAIN, PARTNER, TANTRUM, DISTORT

PAGE 203
UNEARTH, HYGIENE, UNHITCH

PAGE 204
BEARHUG, BLARNEY

PAGE 205
EXOTIC, RUCKUS, DEFLEA, OBEYED

PAGE 206
V: DELVER, LAVISH, ADVERT, CAVORT

PAGE 207
CHEESE, PASTA, POTATO, CLAM

PAGE 208
BALLOT, BLOAT, ALTO, OAT, TO

PAGE 209
UPBEAT, ACTIVE, TEACUP

PAGE 210
DRUNK, DRANK, CRANK, CRANE, REACH, CHEAP

PAGE 211
CELLAR, SINK; VENT, STAIRS; SOCKET, FOYER; PORCH, ATTIC

PAGE 212
WOODED
DECADE
SEWAGE
GOOEY

PAGE 213
1–5; 2–8; 3–6; 4–7

PAGE 214
YOGIC, MUTTON; UNFED, LOOKUP; CYCLE, UGSOME; BRONC, MUSEUM

PAGE 215
NEWBORN, PUBERTY, PERTURB, ENDEMIC

PAGE 216

PAGE 217
CREASE, SKEWED, ENTICE, ATTACK, CAMPUS, GLOBAL, TUSSLE, TYCOON

PAGE 218
COALBIN, CAPTAIN, PLACATE, DETRACT

PAGE 219
GLIMPSE, FILETED, ENLARGE

PAGE 220
ENHANCE, COLLAGE

PAGE 221
HOTROD, UNCLOG, LOGJAM, WEALTH

PAGE 222
B: SOBFUL, SUPERB, BARREN, BECALM

PAGE 223
PARROT or RAPTOR, TURTLE, BEAGLE, LEMUR

PAGE 224
THWACK, WATCH, CHAT, ACT, AT

PAGE 225
ATOMIC, HANDLE, TALCUM

PAGE 226
SHARK, HEARS,

HEART, LATER, LITER, FILET

PAGE 227
MYANMAR, INDIA; EGYPT, RUSSIA; POLAND, ARMENIA; CHILE, GHANA

PAGE 228

PAGE 229
1–4; 2–8; 3–6; 5–7

PAGE 230
DEPTH, VISION; RUGBY, GOPHER; TYPED, VIOLET; UNCLE, TROPHY

PAGE 231
MELODIC, CENSURE, TRISECT, CONTEST

PAGE 232

PAGE 233
ROTATE, DOCTOR, FEDORA, WEAVER, BEDBUG, SAFETY, CLEVER, SAVANT

PAGE 234
BROMATE, PRIMACY, ARMORED, THERMAL

PAGE 235
BYLINES, KILOBIT, COLOGNE

PAGE 236
TENFOLD, UNCLEAN

PAGE 237
WEAKLY, HYBRID, FLAGON, CUTOUT

PAGE 238
C: CHORUS, GLITCH, COEMPT, INFECT

PAGE 239
VILLA, BEACH, RESORT, CRUISE

PAGE 240
METHOD, HOMED, MODE, DOE, DO

PAGE 241
ADRIFT, MYRIAD, TUNDRA

PAGE 242
APPLE, PEARL, TAPER, REPOT, ROUTE, GROUT

PAGE 243
POTENT, WEAK; VALUABLE, TRASHY; PLENTY, SCARCE; FEARFUL, BOLD

PAGE 244

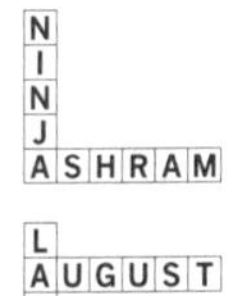

PAGE 245
1–5; 2–7; 3–8; 4–6

PAGE 246
LIMBO, NUGGET; CYNIC, RADIAL; HEDGE, SUMMON; DOILY, JUNIOR

PAGE 247
REVELRY, SERPENT, RIFLERY, OURSELF

PAGE 248

PAGE 249
SLOUCH, PUBLIC, SUGARY, RANCID, UNEASY, BARIUM, UPLAND, SEPTIC

PAGE 250
STANDEE, PENDANT, TENSELY, SUNLAMP

PAGE 251
GENETIC, CROUTON, BOREDOM

PAGE 252
SUCTION, GUMDROP

PAGE 253
PONCHO, OBJECT, NORDIC, BECKON

PAGE 254
P: PROMPT, PRUNED, SPIRAL, UPBEAT

PAGE 255
RETINA, PALATE, ANKLE, EYELID

PAGE 256
ROOMIE, ROMEO, ROOM, MOO, OM

PAGE 257
FRUGAL, MOOLAH, MYOPIA

PAGE 258
THIEF, EIGHT, LEGIT, GLIDE, LODGE, GODLY

PAGE 259
WEIRD, STRANGE; GORGEOUS, LOVELY; DESIGN, CREATE; PLAIN, SIMPLE

PAGE 260

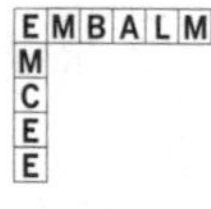

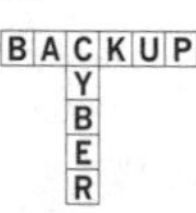

PAGE 261
1–8; 2–7; 3–6; 4–5

PAGE 262
BOOED, TWENTY; RATIO, RUEFUL; MULCH, UNHURT; FLUID, UPROOT

PAGE 263
WEIRDER, SULFIDE, WHERETO, PENSIVE

PAGE 264

PAGE 265
COARSE, SUNTAN, BEATEN, TENANT, PIGLET, PACKET, RADIUS, CINDER

PAGE 266
LETDOWN, ZESTFUL, WITLESS, MOONLIT

PAGE 267
ALMANAC, SIMILAR, DEMONIC

PAGE 268
POLECAT, MODICUM

PAGE 269
COUSIN, NEWBIE, UNFAIR, HOORAH

PAGE 270
M: MORGUE, RESUME, MORASS, SALMON

PAGE 271
BOTTLE, CARTON, POCKET

PAGE 272
MILDEW, WIELD, DELI, LEI, EL

PAGE 273
TARGET, HAMLET, NATURE

PAGE 274
LYMPH, IMPLY, IMPEL, PRIME, VIPER, JIVER

PAGE 275
GABLE, LEIGH (*Gone With the Wind*); BOGART, BERGMAN (*Casablanca*); SWAYZE, MOORE (*Ghost*); *DICAPRIO, WINSLET* (*Titanic*)

PAGE 276

PAGE 277
1–7; 2–5; 3–8; 4–6

PAGE 278
APPEAR, BATMEN; COLLAR, SEAWAY; SYNTAX, FACTOR; CREAMY, AUTUMN

PAGE 279
CARETAKE, AMNESIAC, GARDENIA, WARPLANE

PAGE 280

PAGE 281
BEGONIA, AFFRONT, BUOYANT, DUNGEON, PARAGON, DEADPAN, DELIRIA, BELLHOP

PAGE 282
BENEATH, CATHODE, ENCHAIN, HEADFUL

PAGE 283
TOREADOR, PRINTOUT, NAPOLEON

PAGE 284
MAGICIAN, ARMCHAIR

PAGE 285
AIRSICK, NUCLEUS, BACKLOG, WILDCAT

PAGE 286
F: FLATBED, DEFACED, FAINTLY, CONFESS

PAGE 287
REALITY, PAGEANT, COMEDY, ACTION

PAGE 288
CONCEAL, CANCEL, LANCE, ACNE, CAN, AN

PAGE 289
LAGGARD, GRANOLA, BREADTH

PAGE 290
QUACK, CAULK, LUCKY, BULKY, BULLY, BELLY

PAGE 291
BASSOON, GUITAR; CLARINET, CELLO; TRUMPET, PIANO; ACCORDION, HARP

PAGE 292

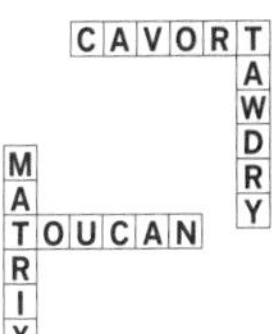

PAGE 293
1–4; 2–7; 3–6; 5–8

PAGE 294
UNWRAP, FACIAL; AGENDA, CACTUS; GAZEBO, ORATOR; GAMBOL, WARMUP

PAGE 295
MEMBRANE, FIREBALL, BESTIARY, AUDIENCE

PAGE 296

G
L
HOOT
V MAD
ZEBRA

PAGE 297
PREFACE, ENCLOSE, AGITATE, COMEDIC, ENNOBLE, ERUDITE, ASCETIC, PRIVACY

PAGE 298
WASTAGE, RAWHIDE, RENEWAL, WIRETAP

PAGE 299
TIDINESS, ENTIRETY, SALIENCE

PAGE 300
PARALYZE, SHEPHERD

PAGE 301
GARBAGE, CHIMNEY, ALREADY, HOODLUM

PAGE 302
V: BRAVADO, DEVIANT, VIRTUAL, CONVERT

PAGE 303
CATFISH, HALIBUT, FLOUNDER, MACKEREL

PAGE 304
HANGOUT, NOUGAT, GAUNT, TUNA, ANT, AT

PAGE 305
ACHIEVE, SUNBATH, EYEBALL

PAGE 306
CIVIC, CIVIL, LIVID, VALID, DAILY, BADLY

PAGE 307
MYSTERY, NOWHERE ("Magical Mystery Tour," "Nowhere Man"); MADONNA, TICKET ("Lady Madonna," "Ticket to Ride"); ELEANOR, WALRUS ("Eleanor Rigby," "I Am the Walrus"); FRIENDS, GARDEN ("With a Little Help from My Friends," "Octopus's Garden")

PAGE 308

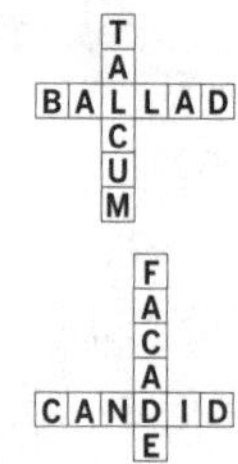

PAGE 309
1–5; 2–6; 3–7; 4–8

PAGE 310
BEFALL, MADCAP; SUBPAR, CANOLA; HANKIE, PEANUT; MISHAP, KEYPAD

PAGE 311
FACTORED, DYNASTIC, POSTCARD, ELEGANCE

PAGE 312

PAGE 313
THEREBY,
CONTEST,
BOMBAST,
DULLISH,
TARNISH,
THYSELF,
SHAKEUP,
SHELLAC

PAGE 314
MAILMAN,
AGENDUM,
MAUDLIN,
ALCHEMY

PAGE 315
SCOLIOMA,
SEAFARER,
SIDELINE

PAGE 316
PHARMACY,
SHANGHAI

PAGE 317
PUTDOWN,
SOFABED,
BASEMAN,
TITANIC

PAGE 318
H: CHIFFON,
CATHODE,
HEADFUL, UNLEASH

PAGE 319
WARTHOG,
CHIPMUNK,
ANTEATER,
CROCODILE

PAGE 320
CARTOON,
RACCOON, ACORN,
ROAN, NOR, ON

PAGE 321
TRAFFIC,
PANICKY,
CARPOOL

PAGE 322
HOTEL, LATHE,
LATER, GLARE,
ARGUE, AUGUR

PAGE 323
LONGBOW, RIFLE;
GRENADE, CLUB;
MUSKET, SABRE;
BAYONET, PISTOL

PAGE 324

PAGE 325
1–6; 2–7; 3–5; 4–8

PAGE 326
OUTACT, SESAME;
GOALIE, SHADOW;
WALRUS, BEDPAN;
COBALT, FAMISH

PAGE 327
OUTREACH,
CLARINET,
CORNMEAL,
TYPECAST

PAGE 328

PAGE 329
GASTRAL,
CENTRAL,
REFRAME,
CUTICLE,
CHAIRED,
CHAOTIC,
DURABLE,
RECEIVE

PAGE 330
UPREACH,
GODHEAD,
ARMHOLE,
MENORAH

PAGE 331
SLOVENLY,
SPHEROID,
STAIDEST

PAGE 332
HANGNAIL,
MARITIME

PAGE 333
ICEBERG,
LADYBUG,
GUMDROP,
ABSTAIN

PAGE 334
W: BYELAWS,
RAWHIDE,
WARMEST,
SWERVED

PAGE 335
SUNBLOCK,
FRISBEE,
UMBRELLA,
SWIMSUIT

PAGE 336
FEDERAL, DEAFER,
FREED, REEF,
ERE, RE

PAGE 337
ADENOID,
FEDERAL,
PREPAID

PAGE 338
KOOKY, COOKY,
CROOK, COLOR,
CORAL, CRAWL

PAGE 339
SPINACH, OLIVE;
TOMATO, CHERRY;
RADISH, ORANGE;
WATERMELON,
PLUM

PAGE 340

PAGE 341
1–3; 2–6; 4–7; 5–8

PAGE 342
IMPACT, ANKLET;
LETHAL, TRAGIC;
LAWMEN, ADROIT;
GASKET, ADVICE

PAGE 343
FRACTION,
NORMALCY,
PROTRACT,
DEADLINE

PAGE 344

PAGE 345
ADAPTOR,
SLEIGHT,
ABALONE,
LANGUOR,
SLOWEST,
COLOGNE,
THICKET,
THEREBY

PAGE 346
NASCENT,
TENFOLD,
ENDMOST,
PUNDITS

PAGE 347
STRATEGY,
ANTILEAK,
ASBESTOS

PAGE 348
LAVATORY,
HONEYDEW

PAGE 349
PRODIGY,
HAIRCUT,
SCANDAL,
VICEROY

PAGE 350
B: SHERBET,
BREADTH,
BREATHE, AMBIENT

PAGE 351
MERCURY, SILICON, TITANIUM, CHLORINE

PAGE 352
DAYLONG, DANGLY, GLAND, DANG, AND, AD

PAGE 353
EARDRUM, PREHEAT, OUTRIDE

PAGE 354
CRYPT, PARTY, TARDY, TREAD, AIRED, ADIEU

PAGE 355
LICORICE, FUDGE; SHERBET, PASTRY; CUPCAKE, PUDDING; TIRAMISU, CANDY

PAGE 356

PAGE 357
1–4; 2–7; 3–6; 5–8

PAGE 358
TRAUMA, ACCRUE; SONATA, CARDIO; BODEGA, ACTUAL; AFLAME, AUGUST

PAGE 359
TIDELAND, ANSWERED, TRADEOFF, MIDRANGE

PAGE 360

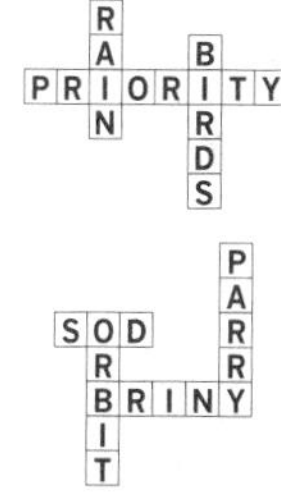

PAGE 361
CRYSTAL, CROWBAR, FACULTY, INVALID, WAYLAID, DUALITY, DRAPERY, DROPLET

PAGE 362
ARMLOAD, HANDGUN, STADIUM, ROTUNDA

PAGE 363
BESTOWAL, CASCADED, BETRAYAL

PAGE 364
BEDSHEET, MOLECULE

PAGE 365
TRICKSY, COPILOT, ANYBODY, BIOTECH

PAGE 366
C: DETRACT, CHEAPEN, CAPTURE, ECSTASY

PAGE 367
POLICEMAN, BRICKLAYER, FISHERMAN, PRESIDENT

PAGE 368
ELEGANT, NEGATE, EATEN, TEEN, NET, EN

PAGE 369
GUMDROP, REVENGE, HEROINE

PAGE 370
NINNY, TINNY, NIFTY, FLINT, FILET, FLUTE

PAGE 371
Michael PHELPS (swimming), Hank AARON (baseball); Peggy FLEMING (ice-skating), Jesse OWENS (track); Roberto CLEMENTE (baseball), Muhammad ALI (boxing); Lance ARMSTRONG (cycling), Nastia LIUKIN (gymnastics)

PAGE 372

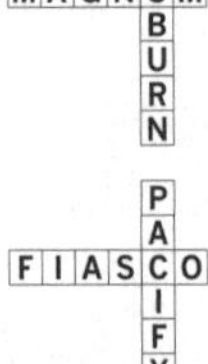

PAGE 373
1–4; 2–6; 3–8; 5–7

PAGE 374
CLAMOR, VASSAL; LEGACY, MISADD; EMBARK, CAPFUL; MAGNET, PRIMAL

PAGE 375
HANDSOME, STEADILY, TRAVESTY, BIRDFEED

PAGE 376

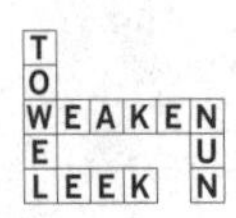

PAGE 377
CADAVER, GRATIFY, BLUNTER, FORTUNE, METHANE, COMFIER, GRANULE, BLOSSOM

PAGE 378
BREWAGE, AGELESS, ALGEBRA, OGREISH

PAGE 379
CATACOMB, CEMETERY, CERULEAN

PAGE 380
FORENSIC, SICKROOM

PAGE 381
TRACHEA, CORDIAL, PHYSICS, SEISMIC

PAGE 382
M: GRIMACE, SANCTUM, PRIMATE, EMBROIL

PAGE 383
CACTUS, STINGRAY, SCORPION, LIGHTNING

PAGE 384
THEREOF, HERETO, ETHER, THEE, THE, EH

PAGE 385
ENTITLE, UMPTEEN, HELPFUL

PAGE 386
UVULA, USUAL, LAUDS, SCALD, CODAS, DOCKS

PAGE 387
Don RICKLES, Lily TOMLIN; Robin WILLIAMS, George CARLIN; Adam SANDLER, Steve MARTIN; Bob NEWHART, Charlie CHAPLIN